The Structure of Perseverance!

Stanley Slaczka

ISBN 979-8-88540-272-9 (paperback)
ISBN 979-8-88540-273-6 (digital)

Copyright © 2022 by Stanley Slaczka

All rights reserved. No part of this publication may be reproduced, distributed, or transmitted in any form or by any means, including photocopying, recording, or other electronic or mechanical methods without the prior written permission of the publisher. For permission requests, solicit the publisher via the address below.

Christian Faith Publishing
832 Park Avenue
Meadville, PA 16335
www.christianfaithpublishing.com

Printed in the United States of America

INTRODUCTION

Perseverance! How do I get perseverance? What do I do to get perseverance? Where should I start to get you started?

Your first tool is to write things down! Your signature is a powerful statement. Your signature is all three things: identity, ego, and superego! Everything you write down is all three things: identity, ego, and super-ego! You remember by writing things down! You remember if you write things down! You remember it better if you write down! Writing things down is powerful! If you think positive—that when you write it down that it's powerful—it will be powerful!

I am going to give you tools to have perseverance! Writing things down is your first tool.

Your surroundings are as important as writing things down. That is your second tool. I will discuss surroundings thoroughly. Your surroundings can be the perfect storm against you, not making you able to have perseverance! Your surroundings can also be the perfect storm for you to have perseverance.

Eating healthy is your third tool. You got to be healthy to have perseverance. You can be disabled and still have all the perseverance you need. If you're a tree and your soil has toxins in it, you need to change the soil to a soil without toxins so your leaves begin to work again!

Your fourth tool is thinking triangularly. The shape of nature is triangular. The Fibonacci triangle is in nature like flowers and fractals. Ask any good contractor that builds buildings; the triangle is the strongest structure. Everything has three in it, like the triangle. A matrix has three in it: an input, an output, and a solution. Music has the triangle in it. Our flag, when folded up, is a triangle. Pyramids are triangular. Nature is triangular. Here is an example of three: 2 + 1 = 3! See three, the number, it's like a triangle, so math starts out triangular. Think triangular. You have one thing, so to figure out the second thing, I get the solution! You want solutions? You write down all three premises. Keep everything in threes. Lists of premises can be put in threes. Organization is the key to success. I love being organized. To have perseverance, you got to be organized—that has to do with your surroundings. If you want, organize everything into triangles; this might help you to be organized.

THE STRUCTURE OF PERSEVERANCE!

Write down what your surroundings are. I will give you tools to identify what your surroundings are. Identify, identify, identify! What is the premise? What angles are you coming at me with? Write them down. What you're trying to figure out is a "Where you are at and what are you in" list!

Here is a list of angles and premises of a "where are you at and what are you in" list.

*Note: If, you can identify these you will be that one step ahead!

1. People talking loudly or screaming
2. People that talk long and professional
3. I call it decoy training.
4. The opposite gender
5. People in front of you or people you are aware of with a clipboard, notebook, or computer writing down every motion they do.
6. Eye witnessing somebody saying "They trained or taught this group of things like horses, people, or something bigger than you!"
7. Heavy losses
8. People claiming that they are in control of something that you're actually in control of
9. Being detained, somebody holding you from going somewhere, a waiting room in

which they say, "Have a seat, get comfortable, make yourself at home!"
10. Somebody showing you their library, their life story, things that they fixed, or things that they control
11. Somebody who claims that you are not what you think you are, that your schooling is not good enough, that you have no schooling, tries to make you look hebetudinous, explains your failures to you. (I'm sure Einstein forgot his umbrella once or twice!)
12. Everything that you reach for and is broken, everything that you imagine is broken. Your missions, operations, and objectives are broken and are breaking up. They show you things that they violently broke.
13. Somebody who says they are in charge of one of your echelons, dimensions, realms, or even you.
14. While you are eating with somebody and they use food angles and premises on you. Their plate or glass is bigger than yours. They have better food than you do. They deliberately give you the wrong food.
15. A person who gradually talks from a regular voice level to a lower voice level, where you

basically can't hear them, like a gradually narrowing tunnel.

16. Somebody shows you the death of something that is your job, death of a person who has the same job as you, death of something in your dimension, realm, sector, family, friends, or group that you belong too
17. A person who takes your signature and says they are in charge of you, a dimension or realm of yours. A salesman with a brief case gets your signature on their calendar then opens and closes their brief case; like the peek-a-boo game, it captures your attention.
18. Somebody who has more clout than you, which explains the person won't tolerate something that you do.
19. A professor, the aura
20. Any type of media, a newsletter, a memorandum, a set of rules, anything that you read, a painted picture that is constructed to affect you. Something creative that has charisma and sculpts you and it can be universal—that means affects all objects with charisma.
21. Seeing doubles of anything that your connected to, your vehicles, people who look like other people, doubles of anything you own, and anything coincidental.

22. The angles of your buddies and friends!
23. Your environment, dimensions, realms—what is in your area? Think triangular! Spheres have triangles in them!
24. Motionless martial arts and butterfly effects!
25. Chaos
26. Faceless enemies, the mysticism of faceless enemies
27. The bottomless pit gags
28. Colors
29. Conformity
30. Morale of your environment

*Note: If you memorize this list, you will have perseverance!

*Note: Each word in this list is a category, and you can make a list to each category! Doing this will get you to isolate problem areas!

* Note: A way to isolate problem areas is to label them into a category of psychological warfare and political warfare! Psychological warfare is words and political warfare is a visual, like a painting, picture, or physical object. Objects have charisma; everything has charisma! Labeling them is like stepping through a minefield. As you label them, you're taking a step through the minefield! Isolate the problems. Make lists.

CHAPTER 1

Build an organized memory with organized thoughts. Everything has a file, everything has a folder—mnemonics, schematics! A mnemonic is something or an image that reminds you of another word or object. The mega memory course is an awesome course I listened to that explains mnemonics and how to use them for a better memory. To have a better memory, you got to eliminate the toxins out of the soil of your tree. Eliminate the fog out of your memory. Create mnemonics, labels, name files, lists, isolate the problem areas. Making lists makes mnemonics and memory files.

It's a way to remember something that you forgot! Write down on a piece of paper a word or picture that might help you remember what you forgot; in essence, what you write down on the paper is a possible mnemonic, a file name. Put this note of a word or picture on your desk or in plain sight so you can see it. Sleep on it. As you remember more things about what you forgot, you write them down also! Every day you will remember more and more of the things you forgot!

If you have an organized environment, this will eliminate a foggy memory. Everything has a place it should be in to eliminate a foggy memory. If your environment is chaos, you will be in the fog. All rooms should have a list of what is in them. All file cabinets should have a list of what is in them. Your house has an address. Your vehicle should have a list to what is in it. Eliminate the fog! By using the list of "Where you are at and what you are in" you made a list of your environment, your area, your dimension, your realm, your atmosphere the motionless martial arts being used on you, the warfare being used on you! So you organized it to eliminate the memory fog.

How important is the environment of your kids? They live in an organized room, but you live in a mess or a foggy chaos! Do your kids have a good memory? A kid who has an organized room remembers more than a kid who does not have an organized room!

What can you put in your kid's room to have a powerful room? Why don't you put stuff like that in your room? If you have a powerful environment, you will have a powerful brain. What culture does your kid live in? Cultures shape people. They shape

THE STRUCTURE OF PERSEVERANCE!

towns, they shape cities, they shape states, they shape countries, and they shape planets! What is it about where you live? What is in your culture? Make lists! Psychological and political environments are powerful. They control what we are, what we do, how we act, how we handle things, how we come up with solutions, and many more things. Let's write them down. We want efficacy. If we live in chaos, you are in the fog. If you have an efficient system, then you are efficient. If you live in a creative environment, then you are creative. Create a positive environment! I watched a course by Norman Vincent Peale called *The Power of Positive Thinking*. I think it is only on VHS. He talked about things in your environment and other things also! If you think you're terrible, then you're terrible. How do we put a stop to that? Your environment! What's in your environment that makes you feel that way? Write it down, correct it if you can. Paint over it. Steamroll over it. Puncture it. Peirce it. Penetrate it. But how? You write it down. How do we get our kids to think they can learn anything? You surround them with what?

As a first step for you, and if you have kids, try vocabulary! Surround yourself with vocabulary CDs or downloadable vocabulary media that are the sounds of vocabulary! You listen to it like music daily. The course I started with was called "verbal advantage" by Charles Harrington Elster! It teaches you 3,500 words, like 3,500 building blocks and 3,500 tools—a framework and structure you can't deny. Read dictionaries. You got the main dictionary, a law dictionary, a business dictionary, a medical dictionary, and some other specialized dictionaries. Surround yourself with vocabulary. That is how you can get a powerful framework, and your kids can go to school for whatever they want. A powerful vocabulary is where to start. Basically, one of those genius kids said to me, "Every school subject cycles through the main dictionary. If you read the dictionary, it's like you have a degree in every subject, and in a way the main dictionary has every language in it."

The main dictionary has the main language diagram on the inside cover—at least, the old dictionary does! If your environment is vocabulary, a lot of things happen. You listen to people who speak clearly. There's no fog, you eliminate memory fog, you can use the dictionary and/or vocabulary media as mnemonics to what you were taught all the way back to when you were born. Yes, each word in the dictionary is a mnemonic to what you were taught all the back to when you were born. Do you have a bad memory? Read the dictionary and use the words you were taught as mnemonics to go all the way back to when you were born. Each word in the dictionary is a mnemonic. Surround yourself with the words you were taught in the dictionary. Learn new words to build new building blocks of a new framework and memory schematics! You will learn to love words! A lot of supreme court justices use dictionaries to write their dissents still today. A lot of speechwriters use the dictionary to write speeches. The way to get something that you want is through communication! How do you communicate? From the words of a dictionary.

People who communicate effectively and efficiently get far in life. They are looked up to. You can say one word and it means a paragraph of words. Your brain will have a stronger structure for communicating to get what you want. Eliminate the brain fog with clear-speaking speakers of vocabulary. A way to stay out of the fog is to read with a dictionary right by your side. The building block of a dictionary work like this: when you say "I'm going to my cave, my chamber, or my library to figure things out," you think of your dictionary as the mnemonic; it's the center to everything you know! All thinking schematics build off that. The schematics are linked to the center of the dictionary, but what mnemonics are linked to is the dictionary! You are like a big schematic, a triangular schematic, a pyramid schematic that can be in a sphere—a complete sphere schematic, a tree of knowledge. Use it to solve the force, the vehicle, the other movie that is going on in your life. Never forget what makes you. Never forget who you are.

To get perseverance, start by writing down your objectives. I said this before: writing down things with a pen is a part of your identity, ego, and superego! Sigmund Freud discovered those three intricate parts: identity, ego, and superego! I'm saying that when you write things down, it must have all three intricate parts in your writings, which must have a lot of emotions and feelings behind it. Write down on paper with a pen.

Now that you got your objectives written down, think big with your objectives. Make a list of how many degrees you want and what the areas are. Write down every interest you have. Don't write down "I have an interest in everything." Isolate the areas and make it a colossal list of everything you're interested in. This is what you do: now that you got your objectives written down, use my list of angles and premises of the "Where you are at and what are you in" list. Use the whole list, and you can expand on that list. To figure out how your environment is trying to stop you from doing your lists, isolate these angles and premises of how forces are trying

THE STRUCTURE OF PERSEVERANCE!

to stop you. It's like walking through a minefield. Identify what that mine is and what that force is that is stopping you!

You might not have perseverance unless you identify the forces that are stopping you. Make a sandbox and design sand tables and put things in your sandbox that simulate the forces you're up against! If it's a decoy, put in your sandbox a symbol of an object that has the charisma of a decoy. Label each item in your sandbox, whether it is psychological warfare or political warfare. Imagine being in your sandbox and identifying the obstacles. You hit a decoy, somebody shows you a picture of the opposite gender, you reach for a broken doorknob; it's wall after wall, and then you hit a bottomless pit. That equation makes you stop in your tracks. Identify what is stopping you and write it down! Divide and conquer it. Break it down, put it on paper. Search your library to overcome this equation. You now have the tools to overcome these obstacles. How do you search your library? Do the seven-day test, where for seven days you shut down all media, all telephones, no music—nothing! You sit in an organized room, so you can think clearly with no fog. Clutter is fog! You knock off the dust!

What are some things you can stick in your room? Stick a globe in your room. Have a dictionary in your room. Put a world map and a country map on your wall. Put a bookcase in your room with books. Put office equipment in your room. How about a poster with a powerlifter with the appropriate gender? A picture album of your life? A notebook to write notes and lists? Put Lego blocks in your room or a chess game, which is mathematical, in your room. Put a lot of mathematical board games in your room! Have a box of a puzzle in room. Put a calculator in your room and use it. Put note boards on your walls in your room. Put a file cabinet in your room. How about what should be in your file cabinet? Let's put some icing on this cake. How about put in your room a bowl with cans of soup with the charisma coming off the bowl and cans of soup with a message saying "Make some soup. Put some spices in the soup, a little of this spice, a little of that spice, and a variety of spices creative spices!"

Grow up with messages like that in your room. Make some interesting files in your file cabinet like

1. A file that says "memory files"
2. A file called "heavy losses"
3. A file that is a list of your friends and family and name it as such
4. A file, named "faceless enemies and mysticism"

5. A file that has every zip code on the planet
6. A file that has every area code on the planet
7. A file, with a 180-year calendar called "the Wall of Life"
8. A notebook for your file cabinet called "the Notebook of Life"
9. A file called "my lists"
10. Put a file in your file cabinet that has a list of books that you have read.
11. A file for art
12. A file that has your list of interests
13. A file for a list for your studies
14. A file, that has a list of all states and their capitals
15. A file of a list of all the presidents' names, vice presidents' names, and the years they were president
16. A file that says "make some soup!"
17. A file that says "tools"
18. A file that says "devices"

*Note: Doing the things in this book will help you.

*Note: By organizing your tools, every time you reach for a tool, it will be right there in a billionth of a second, right where you left it—your life depends on it!

On your note boards in your room, put these items:

1. A paper that lists the years you completed each grade in school
2. A copy of each report card of every year you have been in school
3. A list of all the books you have read
4. A list of the three words that you copied from each page of the dictionary, the first word of each page, the middle word of each page, and last word of each page of the dictionary
5. A list of all the states and capitals
6. A list of all the presidents' names, vice presidents' names, and the years they were president
7. A list of the Roman numeral system symbols
8. A time table of years
9. Names of the places of numbers like ones, tens, hundreds, thousands, hundred thousands, millions, billions, trillions, zillions—as high as it goes!
10. The periodic table!
11. The English system to the metric system of conversions
12. The mathematical formulas
13. The geometry formulas

14. The algebra 1 formulas
15. The algebra 2 formulas
16. The pre-calculus formulas
17. The calculus 1 formulas
18. The calculus 2 formulas
19. The calculus 3 formulas
20. The lyrics of songs, hymns, prayers, or something like the Pledge of Allegiance
21. The list in this book called the "Where you are at and what you are in" list
22. Any of the lists in this book on your note boards

*Note: Doing the things in this book will turn you into a much more intelligent person.

You surround yourself with mnemonics of your past, the mnemonics of what you were taught at the earliest age possible. Each syllable, each word is a mnemonic to your past. When you stare at papers filled with information on your note boards in your file cabinet, you stare at your past. They are the mnemonics to your past. When you stare at objects, you are staring at mnemonics to your past! Objects have charisma and are mnemonics to your past! Objects and words have an aura and charisma. Pick these up put them in your hands. Examine these things closely. A mnemonic is almost like a bridge. These objects, words, or semantics bridge you to what you need to remember. Semantics is important to understand. It's what you emotionally feel and visualize. If I say the word *tree*, you might think of an oak tree in your front yard, and I will be thinking of a maple tree in mine. See how we both picture different pictures? This is what makes communication so hard. You remember a certain set of things depending on how it is said, the tone in which it is said, how you emotionally feel they said it, how fast or slow it is said, how loud or quiet it is said, and how it is emphasized when said. The attorney led the witness into saying that. With what though? Semantics. Have you ever talked to somebody who does not lead you on at all. It's like talking to a robot. How do remember what you need to know in that situation. You actively insert semantics into the robot talking, so you can remember what the robot wants you to know, but what if you're wrong? You need practice at it. If you have ten different semantics to remember one thing, that one thing will be a strong memory, versus having only one semantic to remember that one thing. Use a variety of semantics to remember that one thing: you will have a stronger tree.

CHAPTER 2

There was a test done with flash cards. There were one thousand flash cards with a thousand different types of pictures. They showed all one thousand flash cards to people in a few seconds. The people, when reshown the pictures, recognized 68 percent of the pictures. Subliminal messages do exist. You are a compiled pyramid stack of subliminal messages. You are a sphere of subliminal messages. You have got to think positive, that you have a good memory. Everybody has some type of photographic memory. Peruse a dictionary page by page. Just read a couple things from each page. Take a few days perusing or looking at each page of the dictionary. Spend several seconds on each page reading from a couple spots on each page. Make a notebook. Your notebook has the first word of each page, the middle word of each page, and the last word of each page. The words you are putting in your notebook are mnemonics to the pages in the dictionary. Just by doing this, you actually say, "I probably did see that word before."

When you go deep in thought, you think about the dictionary and what you did looking at the dictionary and reading things from each page of the dictionary. You can do this with a lot of books. Your brain comprehends things at a much faster rate and speed than anybody can speak! You can have the fastest talker in the world and your brain comprehends things faster than he speaks. Your brain comprehends things faster than what your television or media stream broadcasts. The broadcasting speed is not faster than your brain. If you read, watch, and hear things too slow, during the gaps, your brain daydreams and infers the wrong thing to what the real person is saying. The same thing happens when you read. If you read too slow, your brain daydreams and infers the wrong semantics. If you read things too slow or hear things too slow, your brain misunderstands what is being said or read. Your brain fills the gaps of pause with misinformation. The faster you read, the quicker you get the writer's complete thought, and this will curtail your brain's imagination of the wrong semantics or cognitive dissonance.

Some physiology on the brain: your neurons are constantly firing at a billionth of a second! Think of it this way: in order to remember something, your neurons have got to fire the exact same way as they did when you learned those semantics. The amygdala is the part of the brain that deals with emotions and feelings. The amygdala helps with semantics. Semantics are a mnemonic that help you remember what you forgot. The hippocampus is the memory part of the brain. The amygdala and hippocampus have got to communicate with each other to remember things. If you have inflammation and toxins in your body and brain, you will have a lot of cognitive dissonance; your neurons will not fire correctly. Neurons fire like an electrical charge. If you have inflammation and toxins in your body and brain, your neurons will be up against those resistances of toxins; when they try to fire, they could fire incorrectly. You want all parts of your brain to communicate with other parts of the brain correctly. Inflammation and toxins will prevent parts of the brain from communicating with other parts of the brain.

Let me talk about pathology a little bit. Pathology seems like an evil word, but sometimes you need to be pathological to remember what you forgot. Pathology means your brain neurons fire exactly the same way and you do the same thing over and over. Guess what; in order to remember something, your brain neurons need to fire the same way. To have perseverance, your brain needs to fire the same way. Sometimes you do need to be pathological, especially if it is for a good cause. To have perseverance, your brain needs to fire the same way; you cannot have perseverance with your brain firing one way and communicating in another way. How do you do that? I'm giving you the tools to do that. You should not do it for illegal things over and over or do them at all. The tools in this book should be permanently etched in your brain if you want perseverance.

Neurological, biological-chemistry are enzymes and neurochemicals in your brain. You also have the biology of your body. If you have too many toxins in your brain and body, your neurons will fire erratically, and the wrong chemicals or enzymes will fire also. This is why you need to eat and feed the tree with the right foods. Changing the soil of the tree can get the leaves to work again properly. Following a regular detoxing diet is a necessity. It is necessary for your memory; perseverance; a long, healthy life; and a good working brain and body. A good detoxing diet is a necessity. A good way to start out is probably through an elimination diet. I'm not a chiropractor with schooling on functional medicine nor a chiropractor who knows that functional medicine and whole body medicine can coach you better. In my opinion, those types of doctors are more important than a regular doctor, but why aren't they your primary care physician, and why aren't they on your medical insurance? How do you pick a chiropractor for functional medicine and whole-body medicine? What about a chiropractor who does inflammation tests for starters, a chiropractor who is for organic foods. This is how wealthier people have an edge. They can afford to have a functional medicine and whole-body doctor.

Wealthier people have zero problem buying organic foods because they are expensive. Organic foods are a cleaner food and freer of toxins, meaning there are hardly any toxins. I challenge you to do a test: eat organic salads and organic salad dressing at least once a day for a month, and then try a regular salad after one month of organic salads and organic dressings. You will taste the difference.

Some biology of having toxins in your body and biology: your body steals from enzymes to fight the toxins causing inflammation and many things like exhaustion and fatigue. You don't want fatigue or exhaustion if you want perseverance. Having toxins in your body and biology also causes inflammation. Inflammation has probably the longest list in causes of death out of all of the lists and as to other causes to other illnesses. You basically can say inflammation is the cause of everybody's death. Having a diet that fights inflammation from toxins is a must. Being on a detox diet does not always mean you are detoxing from drugs and alcohol. So being pathological can actually be an extremely good thing. Say you want to learn how to play the drums, guitar, piano, or any musical instrument? Then it's okay to have perseverance and be pathological to learn how to play an instrument. This goes with learning how to speed-read. This goes with keeping your house clean. This goes with being organized. This goes with wanting to be a lawyer in school. This goes with wanting to be a sanitation worker or garbage worker. This goes with wanting to write your own book. This goes with wanting to be an artist. This goes with wanting to be a genius. This goes with wanting to be a bodybuilder or powerlifter. This goes with staying in the military for twenty to fifty years. This goes with having the same job for twenty to fifty years.

Then it's extremely important to be pathological. Being pathological is like being in a coma. Having perseverance is like being in a coma. Therefore, being in a coma of perseverance can be an extremely good thing. Does the military need to be in a coma of perseverance to win a war? In the military, you have missions, operations, and objectives that you must complete or else one person might die or many, many people might die, or your country might become tyrannical and full of socialism. At that point, you would need a new country. If the military is not pathological, you would not have a country at all. If you did not have a military, you would not have law at all. But if you're a person that can separate conducting things legally from being illegal and pathological, you are on the right path. If you can consciously figure out what is pathological and what is not pathological, you are on the right path.

CHAPTER 3

I actually want to make you pathological with perseverance. By using the list of angles and premises that I gave you in this book, it will work! I need to break down the list of thirty angles and premises better to give you more information about each angle and premises! To give you more tools with these angles and premises, note the following:

1. These angles and premises are *obstacles!*
2. These angles and premises break your concentration and lead you in a different direction.
3. These angles and premises can make you paranoid; this applies to even the ones that are not actually listed for that angle and premise.
4. These angles and premises make you lose sight of your future; they make you concentrate on these obstacles more than your future objectives.

THE STRUCTURE OF PERSEVERANCE!

5. Our military actually use this psychological warfare and political warfare of the enemy—that is, things on this list and things not in this list.
6. These angles and premises are part of the "Where you are at and what you are in" **list**.

I suggest you expand on all these angles and premises. Write these down and expand on them. Write other angles and premises down even under the categories of these angles and premises.

Let's start with the first angle and premise—people talking loudly. People talking loudly can put you into a submission of where you are quiet. It can make you talk softly or seem like you're talking softly. It is intimidating when people talk loudly. It can seem like they are inferior and know more than you. They put you into submission. They won because they are more outspoken. You are smaller than them because they are louder than you. It's an obstacle.

Now for the second angle and premise: people who talk long and professionally! They outtalk you, making you feel small. They use a vocabulary that people don't understand. You are not on their level. (This is the reason why reading the dictionary and listening to vocabulary-learning media is important, but it also gives you more structure in your brain; your tree of knowledge is bigger, your connecting schematics in your brain is larger, giving you more mnemonics.) You don't relate to what they are saying, so you don't have much to say about it, so it makes you feel smaller than everyone else. There are defense attorneys who try to make the trial as long as possible, so the jury gets confused and forgets segments of the trial to get the person accused of the crime walk off scot-free! This is an obstacle.

Now for the third angle and premise: decoy training. Getting wrong phone numbers is decoy training. Getting wrong directions to find where you are going is decoy training. Getting wrong directions on how to take something apart and put it back together is decoy training. Driving and coming to a dead-end road is decoy training. Driving and coming to a road that says *Do Not Enter* is decoy training! Going into an area where you abruptly get told "You don't belong here," "You are not welcome here," and "You are not permitted here" is decoy training. Going into an area and gradually learning you are not permitted there is decoy training. Reaching for something that isn't there, contacting somebody, and then that person saying "It's not their job!"—that is a decoy. The things you leave that are unfinished are what I like to call "stop-talking tactics." They stop in the middle of a sentence. They use "scrambled talking." They purposely stutter. That is decoy training. Decoy training makes you feel confused, mixed up, in a dilemma, lost, and in the fog. Seeing a misspelled sign is like reaching for a decoy. It also affects your spelling. A misspelled word is a fog. The emergency broadcasting system breaking through your television and phone is a decoy, that breaks your attention. This is an obstacle.

Now the fourth angle and premise: the opposite gender. You come in some type of contact with the opposite gender. It will make you feel small; it can get your hormones going. The opposite gender captures you or captivates you, and you lose sight of your future and think of a new future. This is an obstacle.

Now the fifth angle and premise: people who are in front of you with a clipboard, notebook, or computer, writing down every motion that you do. They make you feel that they are in charge. This is an obstacle.

Now the sixth angle and premise: witnessing somebody saying they "trained or taught" this group of things, like horses, people, or something bigger than you. This will make you feel small. This is an obstacle.

Now the seventh angle and premise: heavy losses. This can happen to you in a stealthy manner. You come home and notice your tea towel is missing or out of place. You can get paranoid, feel small. The enemy delta forces can do this to you, that's their job! They come in your house, move something like your shoes or a millimeter tilt to the whole picture. This mentally tilts the future you picture your life being. It changes you mentally. It creates a mental fog. Your future is now foggy, like the inside of your house. It makes you feel like something is conspiring against you to where you concentrate on that more than your future objectives. The military can get heavy loses millions of soldiers die making the generals think they will lose. While you are destroying our military over there, we are going to destroy your military by doing this, because we knew our military was going to get destroyed over there. It's a chess game. The problem with this country is we no longer can accept heavy losses. The generals would lose their command if they got heavy losses. If you put 1 million soldiers there, so the enemy will send 3 million to overrun the 1 million you put in that place. It could weaken the enemies' front in another area, making them weak in another area, and you overrun them in their weakened area. It's called strategy. This country can no longer do that,

THE STRUCTURE OF PERSEVERANCE!

because our country is not fierce, like it once was too compassionate. By the way, if something comes up moved in the place where you live or missing in the place where you live, it's like whoever did it is now in charge of you. You lose control of things, and if you are not aware of that, then it is effective. A sudden death in your family is heavy losses. This is an obstacle.

Now the eighth angle and premise: people claiming they are in control of something that you're actually in control of. This can mean something that is a part of you, like something you touched or something that your emotions or feelings are attached to in your dimensions and realms. It can be something that you took apart and put back together. It's an extension of you. Them claiming they are in control of anything, that is an extension of you. They are bigger than you and they control it, so you feel small. This is an obstacle.

Now the ninth angle and premises: being detained, somebody holding you from going somewhere. You are in a waiting room in which they say "Have a seat, get comfortable." For an area where people say "Make yourself at home," my retort is "I prefer to stand. This is an obstacle."

Now the tenth angle and premise: somebody showing you their library, life story, things that they fixed, or things that they control. The library will make them look like they are smarter than you. Their life story will make them look like they are tougher than you. They will have a story where they say "I owned the president's house before the president owned his house." The things that they fixed might be things that you would be able to fix, so you think they will like be able to fix anything. Things that they control could be something as simple as their driving a tractor trailer, a large truck (this is a different type of angle and premise than I trained or taught in the sixth angle and premise), or that they can speed-read. They show you a picture of the pope implying that the pope is more powerful than you and you got to do what the pope says. This is an obstacle.

Now the eleventh angle and premise: somebody who claims that you are not who you think you are, that your schooling is not good enough, that you have no schooling, or tries to make you look hebetudinous and explains your failures to you I. (I'm sure Albert Einstein forgot his umbrella once or twice!) Someone who tells you that they were in the same thing as you were and they didn't learn anything, and they are hebetudinous—they know nothing—this is an obstacle.

THE STRUCTURE OF PERSEVERANCE!

Now the twelfth angle and premise: everything you reach for is broken. Everything that you imagine is broken. Your missions, operations, and objectives are broken and are breaking up. They show you things that they violently broke. An alarm or horn that abruptly starts blasting breaks your attention. A sudden ring from your phone breaks your attention. An alert from social media is a break in your concentration. A sudden urge to look at your phone or television is a break in your concentration. A sudden breaking news story that is associated with one of the items that is an extension of you will break your concentration. Power outages and flickering lights, like you do to your kids to get them to stop what they are doing, and then them saying "We are going to cap this pipeline off!"—this is an obstacle.

Now the thirteenth angle and premise: somebody who says they are in charge of one of your echelons, dimensions, realms, or even you. "I'm in charge of your tree!" They use control words. It's like you are submitting to their control. This is an obstacle.

Now the fourteenth angle and premise: while you are eating, they use food angles on you. Their plate or glass is bigger than yours. They have better food than you. They deliberately give you the wrong food. This is an obstacle.

Now the fifteenth angle and premise: a person that gradually talks from a regular voice level to a level you basically can't hear anymore. It's a gradually narrowing tunnel! Your life seems like it is gradually narrowing. Your missions and operations are gradually narrowing to where you can't get to the objective. This is an obstacle.

Now the sixteenth angle and premise: someone shows you the death of something that is your job, shows you the death of a person, that has the same job as you, shows you the death of something in your dimensions, realms, sectors, family, friends, or group that you belong to. You see the death of something associated with your identity, ego, or superego. This is an obstacle.

Now the seventeenth angle and premise: a person who takes your signature and says they are in charge of you, a dimension or realm of yours. A salesman, lawyer, or police officer with a briefcase gets your signature on his calendar or on his paperwork, opens and closes their briefcase with your signature in it; like a peek-a-boo game, it captures your attention. A person who takes your signature and says they are going to close your file or folder, a person who takes a picture of you and says, "I own

THE STRUCTURE OF PERSEVERANCE!

this picture!"—a picture and signature are all three parts of your identity, ego, and superego—a person who gets you to sit in his office and he has a big fat chair and you get a small chair, which makes you feel smaller than him and your atmosphere—these are obstacles.

Now the eighteenth angle and premise: somebody who has more clout than you, who explains he won't tolerate something that you do, or that he won't tolerate integrity violations or insubordinations, he won't tolerate your flaws—this is an obstacle.

Now the nineteenth angle and premise: a professor or teacher that you have, did have, or will have. Professors and teachers stand in front of you and you think they know everything. Professors and teachers have a very high charisma, they have a glow, they have an aura. The pope has a powerful aura. The president has a powerful aura. Anybody you look up to who can a mentor—your parents, an actor, a person playing sports, or anybody famous—you automatically submit to them. They put you into submission with the greatest of ease. Your leaders are the symbol of numbers 1. This is an obstacle.

Now the twentieth angle and premise: any type of media, a newsletter, a memorandum, a set of rules, anything that you read, a painted picture that is constructed to affect something creative, that has charisma and sculps you, and it can be universal—that means it affects all. Objects have charisma. Now this, a leader who has a newsletter explaining he or she is cutting these people from their position, this action makes them look big. They can say "I cut a bigger tree down than you, I seem to be bigger than you." Say you are passing out a newsletter saying that you're cutting the president from your list of friends—it's big move. You have the charisma of what now? Say you have a newsletter that says you are cutting congressmen's salaries. What charisma do you have now? And I mean you as in the charisma that you have...what aura do you have now? Objects have charisma and people are objects. So what charisma do you obtain? What kind of charisma do you want for yourself? What is the movie you're stuck in? Make your own movie. You are now the linguist, you're the director of the movie, and you are going to make your own movie, train, or vehicle. This is an obstacle.

Now the twenty-first angle and premise: seeing doubles of anything that you are connected to. You vehicles double. Certain people look like other people, doubles of other people, doubles of anything that you own, doubles of any object, divide and conquer, anything coincidental. It makes things a

THE STRUCTURE OF PERSEVERANCE!

blur or foggy, it breaks your concentration. Two trees in your front yard make people get cross-eyed when they stare at your house. This is an obstacle.

Now the twenty-second angle and premise: the angles of your buddies, friends, and family. They take you to restaurants. You eat comfortably with them. You are comfortable with them because you can say anything, so they got you to submit. Your friends and family do you favors. You look up to your friends and family. They hug you. They shake your hands. They raise their hands and wave at you. You have to move for them and wave back. They get you to move here and move there, breaking the realm. They talk down to you. They make you feel honored, they honor you. Friends get you to think you're compatible with things. You should bond with these things. This is an obstacle.

Now the twenty-third angle and premise: your environment, dimension, realms—what is in your area. What is the name of the area you are in, the name of the room you're in, the name of the building you're in, and the name of the town or city you're in? If the name of the group you're in is the equationists, how would you act? You would act like an equationist. Do you see how your environment affects you now? Think triangularly. Spheres have triangles in them. Anything that makes you feel humiliated; anything that affects your feelings or emotions; anything that affects your identity, ego, or superego, the Sigmund Freud theory; and the things that affect that; something you fear—you feel boxed in, so you feel boxed in any way. The military uses the enemy's zodiac signs against the enemy. When the military collects intelligence on the enemy, the military wants to know the enemy's zodiac sign. Here is an example of a tactic used on Leos. I believe they talk to Leos about spots. Leo the Lion, the spots amaze lions. The military also collects data on the enemy's phobias, like a phobia to clowns. A psychological warfare and political warfare operation can be one where the military sends out a clown to the leader of the country that has a phobia to clowns. How does this affect the leader of the country? The military department that sends out a clown to one of the enemy leaders with a phobia to clowns as a means of psychological warfare and political warfare operations is called the psychological warfare department. What are the semantics of your environment? What are substantive angles and premises being used on me? This is an obstacle.

Now the twenty-fourth angle and premise: motionless martial arts and butterfly effects. This is what gives you that gut instinct, but what is giving that gut instinct? How do you know it's just right to

THE STRUCTURE OF PERSEVERANCE!

do this? How do you know that is the right answer? How do you know this is the right path to take? How do you know this is the right thing to write down? The aura itself. You are living in this area in a town in your home country, and a butterfly effect happens in another country over the ocean five thousand kilometers away, and that butterfly effect five thousand kilometers away has an effect on you to do something a certain way. This is an obstacle.

Now the twenty-fifth angle and premise: chaos! Anything not organized is overwhelming. You run from chaos. Clutter, traffic—for anything that does not make sense, always say to yourself you do understand it. If you don't, then you will never understand it. Think positive that you understand everything. Nothing is overwhelming. This is an obstacle.

Now the twenty-sixth angle and premise: faceless enemies—the mysticism of faceless enemies. For anything faceless or mysterious, what you can do is just scribble on a piece of paper and put it in a file and label it *faceless things and enemies*. Anything faceless puts you in a stupor. The mysticism puts you in a stupor. What types of things in your environment are you mystified about? Put a face on it, scribble on paper, and now it has a face. Categorize it and put a face on it. This is an obstacle.

Now the twenty-seventh angle and premise: the bottomless-pit gags. You send letters, and who you send them to is a bottomless pit. The people around you are a bottomless pit! You call somebody about the same issue thirty times, and they are a bottomless pit. What other kinds of bottomless pits are out there. This is an obstacle.

Now the twenty-eighth angle and premise: colors. Colors have an effect on everybody. Your eye has three color spectrums. The three cones in your eye, I believe, are green, red, and blue! Yellow is piercing, red is cutting, blue is perseverance and puts you to sleep with its several meanings, orange is fear, brown settles you down like a log cabin, green gives you deep thought, black makes you aggressive, white claims innocence. Colors can affect people differently but are very similar to what I just described. You learn effects of colors with color codes. You need color codes in a country. Every advanced country has a color code.

Now the twenty-ninth angle and premise: conformity. You blend in. You blend in with your group. You are submissive. It's okay to be submissive at times, but it's an obstacle. You go into a business and see a tip jar, and you confirmed to it to give a tip because of the charisma and aura of the tip jar.

THE STRUCTURE OF PERSEVERANCE!

The tip jar conforms you. Things that catch your eye, you conform to these. This is an obstacle.

Now the thirtieth angle and premise: morale of your environment. You have people around you who drag you down to not complete your mission and objective. Everybody has missions—even nuns have missions. The people around you say "You can't do that!" The morale of your environment is like a blob of what? Break it down into triangular forces—forces of three. What are these forces? Say you want to stay in the military for twenty to fifty years, and all the soldiers around you are all just doing their four-year enlistment and getting out. The soldiers are celebrating that they are getting out in a year. They conform you into just doing your four-year enlistment. If the people around you don't do exercise, then you don't exercise. If people around you don't write books, then you don't write books. If people around you don't go to college, then you don't go to college. You take the lead and make an example and give yourself the morale to do these things that nobody is doing around you! You set an example to have a high morale. You install a new morale to the people around you. Morale means everything. Does the leaders of the military need to think about morale? A military that has morale can defeat anything; they will not lose the battles and the war. Eating right affects morale. Your health affects morale. If you eat these toxic, greasy things, you will have low morale—the grease slows you down.

What are the forces that are stopping you from completing your missions, operations, and objectives? Why doesn't anybody else in your environment want to do the missions, operations, and objectives that you want to do? Why do you let that stop you? They indirectly say things that are forces that stop you from completing your mission and objective. What are these indirect things being said? Doctors say you can never be healed. The people around you put a stop to your morale. They make jokes about your morale. The people make jokes about your character. What kind of morale do you need to run for a government position? Everybody around you hates leaders and leaders of the country; they do nothing but talk about flaws of the people who hold the job they want. You want that job, but the people around do nothing but explain that those people are the lowest form of life. You need strong morale. A mission and objective of yours should be to have high morale.

Use the tools of this book to give you perseverance on having high morale as a mission and objective. Who cares what people think about your

THE STRUCTURE OF PERSEVERANCE!

morale? What are these people saying indirectly? Write it down. Men, how about if the people around you are saying "You are acting like a girl"? Females, how about if the people around you are saying "You are acting like a guy"? For some reason, I'm going to put repeating phrases that mesmerize and hypnotize you under the morale category. Say you are exposed to a phrase like this: "I think Zip's Pizza is the number 1 pizza!" You get mesmerized by that phrase to the point that you do think Zip's Pizza is the number 1 pizza. Anybody who says "I'm going to zip things up in here!" To have a high morale, you must have high self-esteem. Weather affects morale and is an obstacle. Ecosystems affect morale and are an obstacle! Morale affects morale. This is an obstacle.

*Note: A retort for all the categories of these angles, premises, and obstacles of the categories of the thirty angles, premises, and obstacles is to use tools like holding an unframed globe in your hands like a basketball. Rotate the globe in your hands and look down on everybody on the planet. Picture what is stopping you while holding the globe. Picture what is the future of the planet while holding the globe. Meditate with the globe in your hands. Close your eyes and hum with the globe in your hands. Picture what people are doing all over the planet while holding the globe. Hold the globe with your eyes closed and say "There is only one direction, forward!" Think about the paths you can take while holding the globe with your eyes closed. I will try to give you more tools like this.

*Note: Here is another retort to all the categories of these angles, premises, and obstacles: the categories of the thirty angles, premises, and obstacles is the seven-day test where you isolate yourself from all inputs of your life, lock yourself in, make it a green room if possible. I will try to give you more tools like this.

*Note: Here is another retort to all the categories of these angles, premises, and obstacles: the categories of the thirty angles, premises, and obstacles is to stare at a faraway star. I will try to think of more tools like this!

*Note: Here is another retort to all the categories of these angles, premises, and obstacles: the categories of the thirty angles, premises, and obstacles is to kick a rock in a big parking lot and zoom in on the rock with your eyes and focus on the rock while kicking. I will try to give you more tools like this.

*Note: Here is another retort to all the categories of these angles, premises, and obstacles: the categories of the thirty angles, premises, and obstacles is to play darts, focusing on the very tip of the dart

THE STRUCTURE OF PERSEVERANCE!

and aiming and throwing the dart at the dartboard. I will try to give you more tools like this.

*Note: Here is another retort to all the categories of the angles, premises, and obstacles: the categories of the thirty angles, premises, and obstacles is, while everybody is moving, then say "I am going to move like this" (physically say it and visualize it)! I will try to give you more tools like this.

*Note: Here is another retort to all the categories of the angles, premises, and obstacles: the categories of the thirty angles, premises, and obstacles is saying "Big Red 1 coming through!" You visualize yourself as Big Red 1 I will try to give you more tools like this.

You actually do need to form retorts to all of these angles that stop you from completing your missions, operations, and objectives. You address each and every angle and premise with a retort. By addressing each and every angle and premise with a retort, you are putting yourself in a commanding position. You become on top of these angles and premises. You steamroll right over these angles and premises. Picture yourself as yellow steamroller. Picture yourself as 100 percent piercing energy. Picture yourself as a straight arrow. Picture yourself as 100 percent cutting energy. Picture an axe. I am going to give you retorts for each angle and premise right now. They might seem simple, but they will do the job. Some retorts might be repeated in a different angle and premise. You can't think of more on your own. This list is for the list of "where are you at and what are you in" Okay, here are some retorts for each angle and premise:

For angle and premise 1, your retort is to speak louder yourself, maybe even hit a notch or two above their volume level that they use on you.

For angle and premise 2, your retort is to come up with a word that they don't know the definition of.

For angle and premise 3, your retort for decoy training is to have a list of "things to do"! That to-do list is a list of objectives. When you reach the decoy or reach for a decoy, you don't forget what your objective is. You take what is unfinished and you finish it.

For angle and premise 4, your retort for the opposite gender is to copy down a mnemonic that reminds you of how the opposite gender was shown to you. You can copy down the name of the person who was shown to you. Now you own that person of the opposite gender. They are in your prison or sandbox. You can paint the paper with that information on it black. Paint right over it.

THE STRUCTURE OF PERSEVERANCE!

For angle and premise 5, your retort is to copy down things of every motion that they do.

For angle and premise 6, your retort is to visually think of yourself training something bigger than what they said. "They trained!" you say out loud. What is it that you trained that is bigger than what they trained?

For angle and premise 7, your retort is to visually say out loud "That is [heavy loses]!" Put the name of the "heavy losses" in the file you made in your file cabinet and mark it *heavy loses!*

For angle and premise 8, your retort is to say out loud "I'm in control of the planet, the universe, and outer space!"

For angle and premise 9, your retort is to say out loud "I think outside the box!"

For angle and premise 10, your retort is to visualize how big your library is. Think of every book you had in school, everything you ever read, and say "I know my library perfectly well!"

For angle and premise 11, your retort is to say out loud "I know what I am," "I know what I'm capable of," and "If you reach for it, you are ready for it!"

For angle and premise 12, your retort is to look at your objectives on your to-do list.

For angle and premise 13, your retort is to say out loud "I'm in charge of myself!"

For angle and premise 14, your retort is to give yourself a spectacular meal.

For angle and premise 15, your retort is to crank the volume up on your television, car radio, or home radio.

For angle and premise 16, your retort is to say out loud, "I'm still alive, and I'm going to live a long life!"

For angle and premise 17, your retort is to say out loud "I own my signature, I own me, and I'm in control of myself!" You also write your signature down on paper ten times.

For angle and premise 18, your retort is to say out loud "I'm bigger than you!"

For angle and premise 19, your retort is to say out loud "I'm the professor!" Make a template with the word *professor* and your name. Stick a piece of paper in your wallet that says *professor*.

For angle and premise 20, your retort is to say out loud and write down, "I control my destiny," "I'm in control of my environment," and "I make my own media!"

For angle and premise 21, your retort is to say out loud "I am Big Red 1!"

THE STRUCTURE OF PERSEVERANCE!

For angle and premise 22, your retort is to put a list of your friends and family in a file in your file cabinet. They are in your prison, your dungeon!

For angle and premise 23, your retort is to say out loud and write down, "I'm in control of my destiny!" "I'm in control of my environment!" "I'm making a new movie!"

For angle and premise 24, your retort is to say out loud and write down "I'm Big Red 1 coming through!"

For angle and premise 25, your retort is to say out loud and write down "I'm the master organizer!"

For angle and premise 26, your retort is to make a file for your file cabinet that is labeled *Faceless Enemy and Mysticism.*

For angle and premise 27, your retort is to have copies of everything that you sent to the bottomless pit and send copies of your copies to outside forces. If you don't, you get bound up, you will be in a stupor, and this locks you up mentally.

For angle and premise 28, your retort is to concentrate on the forces of colors and work your way through each one that is changing your emotions and feelings toward your objectives.

For angle and premise 29, your retort is writing down *They sucker in then hang you out to dry!*

For angle and premise 30, your retort is to say out loud and write down *I'm the morale master!*

Okay, now I'm going to advance you to a higher level of thinking. This list of thirty categories of angles and premises called the "Where you are at and what you are in" list can come at you with multiple forces and equations all at once, like a perfect storm. I'll make up an equation to one of the multiple forces right now.

[What if your environment comes at you with angle and premise 20? First, your retort should be "I am the media!" and "I'm making this movie!" You start pushing all kinds of forces outward, and then they use the angle and premise 3 on you. The decoy training and everything else is coming to a dead-end, a wall. Then they blast you with angle and premise 27, the bottomless pit of gags.]

Analyze the three parts in that equation I put brackets around, the equation of three different parts. Recognize the directions of the three different forces in the brackets right above this paragraph. Can you figure out how the three different forces affect you, and do you know these three different forces and what they make you do? They used this equation on you to achieve what? The top military leaders use equations like this on the enemy to achieve results from the enemy. It's called psychological warfare and political warfare. Any type of warfare is an act of war. This is why painting a curb the wrong color is an act of war. Painting a fire hydrant the wrong color is an act of war. Destroying a country's color code is internal sabotage and an act of war. Okay, can you imagine six hundred thousand different equations coming at you all at once? This is what your environment is, and I broke it down for you. But guess what, you still have got to identify these forces on your own and write them down also to keep track of what is going in your life right now.

Now make up your own equation with the list of the thirty categories of angles, premises, and obstacles list of "Where you are at and what you are in."

Can you imagine if we named cities in our country to create an equation? Here is an example of a name of their cities: in an equation, the name of the first city is Dots. The name of the second city is Solid, and the name of the third city is Bottomless Pit. Do you see the equation there? First you pass through the city Dots, then you pass through the city of Solid, and then you pass through the city of Bottomless Pit. Now do you see the equation they ran on you?

*Note: After reading this book, you should be confident to be able take on negotiators of foreign countries.

CHAPTER 4

A brain being able to organize thoughts is a brain that has efficacy. Efficacy gives precision, and precision gives speed. In a conversation, you have got to be quick thinking on what you want to retort back to the person talking. How are you going to come up with a retort extremely quickly? Your tools need to be totally organized so when you reach for a tool in your brain, it's right where it was supposed to be organized. Organize thoughts. What can you do to have organized thoughts? You read things that are organized. A dictionary is very organized. You talk like a dictionary? Good. People will be able to comprehend what you say. The origami book *The New World Champion Paper Airplane Book*, written by John M. Collins, is organized with precision writing. Read that book!

The books that are organized can be both easy to remember and hard to remember. They can be easy because one step leads to the next step. A dictionary is flat. What you have got to do with a dictionary is come up with a mnemonic that has feeling and emotions—a mnemonic that has excitement, a mnemonic that has action, a mnemonic that just plain pours out with energy. You need to make those types of mnemonics for this book. You need to live and breathe this book. Okay, now I want to explain a tool that is like a mnemonic tool function. The tool is you deliberately leave an item out where you can find it, and that item reminds you of a book. That's how mnemonics work. It's like a letter in the mail. You can take a hammer and put in a plastic bag and put it behind your shed. When you see this hammer in a plastic bag behind the shed six months from now, it will remind you of this book. Okay, now that you understand that tool, you have got to overuse that tool. Do you see how important mnemonics are now?

Okay, now you got two other lists in this book that go into your file cabinet and your note boards. These items are in your possession—you own them. What is in your file cabinet is what you are in control of, nobody controls you! The files are in something—your file cabinet. Putting things in your file cabinet can be the same action as writing something down that glows; it glows so much that it is stopping you from your objective, and then you paint over the glow with black paint—that will open the path to your objective. You have got to have a high self-esteem to do the things in this book—make that an objective. So you put a variety of things in your file cabinet, things that you want to remember and things that try to stop you from completing your missions, your operations, and objectives. The things on your notebooks are mnemonics of your past, and they are mnemonics of what your missions are, your operations are, and what your future objectives are. The mnemonics on your note boards are like objects; they have charisma.

*Note: You have got to have a high self-esteem to do the things in this book. You can't let things like humiliation stop you for doing the things in this book. You can't let the fear of humiliation stop you from doing the things in this book. You can't let your emotions or feelings stop you from doing the things in this book. It's a test to see if you have what it takes. By passing the test, you will notice you do become more intelligent by doing things in this book. You won't know how more intelligent it makes you unless you do it.

*Note: This book is meant to be read by kids of the youngest age and all ages above that age.

Okay, taking a globe and staring down on it, I really do think you increase your IQ! I want to mention that IQ tests aren't necessarily a creditable test.

THE STRUCTURE OF PERSEVERANCE!

Why is that? Because the test itself asks questions of a knowledge that you have not been exposed to. Suppose you are brought up in a different culture from somebody who has lived in a different city or town. In the culture that you were brought up in, you might have learned more about computers than philosophy. You might say that's not a true; an IQ test is to see if you know a wide range of topics. Well, think about it. A genius in this culture might not know the full culture of Italy. What if you write a book on *How to Raise Your IQ to Genius Level?* This book covers all the areas that are on an IQ test. The IQ test has mostly philosophy and history questions and no questions on your health. So you are considered a genius on philosophy and history, but you know nothing about health. You might be a genius on thirty-six different areas, and the IQ test itself claims you are a genius if you know these thirty-six areas. Who is more of a genius, the person who knows the thirty-six areas that are not on the IQ test, or the one who knows the thirty-six areas that are actually on the test? I would say the genius who does not know the thirty-six areas that are on the IQ test is still a genius.

Okay, so staring down on a globe gets you to think more clearly. It definitely does. So let's add to that. I want everybody who reads this book to add to it on your own. This book will give you common sense to do that. The people who add to this book are the ones who get something out of it on a higher basis. Even if you don't add things to this book, you will still be intelligent to complete your missions, operations, and objectives. I am going to add tools to help you stare down at a globe to make you think more clearly. Okay, go to a high place like a mountain and stare down on everything; this will clear the fog up. Okay, go to a high bridge and stand in the middle of the bridge and stare down on everything; this will clear up the fog. Take a plane ride and get a window seat and stare down on everything; this will clear the fog up. Fight your way through the fog. Use a large knife and wave it in the air to cut through the fog. While waving the large knife in the air and watching it cut through the air, visualize that you are cutting through the fog. Hold the globe in your hands without the globe's framework, which holds it upright as a bare globe—nothing but globe—and spin it in your hands like a basketball, a kickball, and a volleyball. You got the world in your hands. Okay, now I will add this tool. Have a model of the solar system for yourself to look at.

*Note: If you add tools to this book on your own, you will be a higher level, but if you don't, you will still have the max level of perseverance. Your

THE STRUCTURE OF PERSEVERANCE!

cultures are all different, so you will need to write things down, you will need to isolate and identify the forces that you are up against on your own.

*Note: What obstacles are you up against?

Here is another tool to get you through the obstacles, a retort. It is the "in-disguise" tactic. Repeatedly say to yourself out loud "I'm a genius in disguise!" I'm going to add to that; say to yourself repeatedly "I'm a CEO in disguise!" A CEO is a chief executive officer. Another add-on: say to yourself relatedly "I am the chief of police in disguise!"

Another add-on: say to yourself and out loud "I am the governor in disguise!" Another add-on: say to yourself and out loud "I am the president in disguise!" Another add-on: say to yourself and out loud "I am the chief lawyer in disguise!" This is the "in disguise" tactic.

*Note: You can rewrite this book to put it in your permanent memory. When you write things down, it is more powerful than when you don't. A pen is an extension of you on paper—An extension of you because the extension in penwork is an extension of your identity, ego, and superego.

*Note: If this book was taught in schools as a class, everyone would go to college.

Can you imagine if the whole country lived and died by this book? How would it affect the country?

You would have a more intelligent country. The cultures would become more advanced. People would thrive to be intelligent. The devices that are around you would get even more advanced all the faster. Take a person who has no devices around them and compare them to a person who has devices around them. The people who do have devices around are more advanced mentally. Farmers do have devices around them. The cognitive dissonance of the brain is more complex for the people who have devices around them; therefore, since they have all these complicated devices around them, they are conditioned to handle the stresses of overcoming obstacles at a higher level.

Take a person who has the most complex devices in their culture and put them in a culture with no devices at all. What would happen? This is why you need to challenge yourself and listen to things that you think you can't understand. (I'm here to tell you, even though you don't think you can understand complicated things, you actually do!) Farmers do have complicated devices around them. If you surround yourself with complicated patterns, structures, and designs, you can figure other complicated patterns, structures, and designs by using the ones you already know. So push yourself as hard as you can to expose yourself to most complicated things there are. There is a company that I call the Library of Congress that has called the Great Courses. This has college-level courses that you can listen to and watch These courses from the Library of Congress called the Great Courses is about as complicated as you can get. So go from listening to those professors and watching those professors of complicity do everyday common things; it is a drastic change.

I want to talk about health again. If you live in the city, there are a lot of toxins in the air—this is called pollution. These toxins in the air affect how your brain neurons fire. These cause you to have a foggy brain. This is why all people need detox kits. Detox kits from chiropractors and doctors help you against pollution. Okay, if you think that is not necessary, then why is it the people from the city, when they take a vacation in the country areas, say things like "I figure things out when I'm out in the country" or "I think clearer when I'm in the country" or "I feel so much better when I'm on vacation in the country." And they also say "I need to take a vacation in the country, so I can figure things out." I would say the main reason is pollution. But I need to mention again the seven-day test when you go to an area where there are no inputs of things like your television and your phones. You'll want to do the seven-day test in the country with fresh air. You don't have to shut down every factory in the city to have a clean city. You can have a livable city without shutting down every factory in the city. What you need is detox kits from the chiropractor or doctors. If you live in the cities, you are more susceptible to health conditions like heart attacks, strokes, cancer, and diabetes—this has to do with the toxins in the air and the things that you touch. Everybody needs a functional medicine doctor. If you want, you can make the seven-day test a thirty-day test. When I was in the military, I was always out in the middle of nowhere.

Soldiers know how to stay focused, and now I'm giving you the tools to stay focused. How can you stay focused in a room of clutter?

People have an instinct to look for holes. Keep in mind, electrons always flow down the easiest path. People have an instinct to look for trees and buildings. Keep in mind, electrons always flow down the easiest path. This is just plain physics. Do you want to take a hard left or an easy right? If you're a person who only takes the easy right, you are predictable. A person who is in tip-top physical shape has no problem taking the hard left. You have got to be in tip-top condition in both areas—physical shape and mental shape. Your brain is like a muscle. If you don't use the brain, like a muscle, it becomes mush. You listen, watch, and even read the most complicated things to work the muscle called the brain. Your brain is a muscle, and you got to get it pumping by exposing yourself to the most complicated things. That is how you work out the mental side of your body, the way you work out the physical side of your body through weightlifting. You have got to work out both parts of the body, and you have to do this even after you die. You never stop putting yourself through school. Keep your brain muscles pumping or these turn to mush. Everybody gets indolent, torpid, and listless when it comes to working out the brain muscles. Don't shy away from complicated things; take it by the bull's horns and ride it. People don't have the motivation to work out the brain muscles because they have too many toxins in their biology. The toxins make you indolent; toxins are why you have no motivation. Now, when it comes to motivation to working out with weightlifting and cardio, people don't have the motivation to do it because they have too many toxins in their biology; the toxins in their biology makes them indolent, not motivated. How can you have perseverance if you are so overloaded with toxins—you can't even move, are indolent, torpid, and listless. Work those brain muscles. Work your human anatomy muscles. Work those toxins out of you. Get oxygen to your brain. The more oxygen you get to the brain, the more motivation you will have.

CHAPTER 5

"The Memory Process List" is a process to remember things. When you can't remember something, you are in the black! How do you get out of the black?

1. First thing you do is go through the alphabet (A through Z).
2. You go through each letter of the alphabet and try to figure out a word a letter starts with.
3. What does the word sound like? What does that word remind you of? You write down that word.
4. That is your building block. Even if that word has nothing to do with the real word, you're still trying to remember.
5. Try to figure out the shape of what you're trying to remember.
6. Try to write down on a piece of paper the shape of it, even if you just came up with a scribble.

THE STRUCTURE OF PERSEVERANCE!

7. Think positive that you can do it.
8. You will struggle, you will let out grunts and screams.
9. Okay, now relax; relaxing is the most important part of it all.
10. Let your mind drift off of it.
11. You have something written down that is a mnemonic to what you want to remember, so you won't forget that you need to remember it.
12. Go to other things in your life.
13. Peruse your computer.
14. Peruse your television.
15. Peruse your books.
16. Peruse the dictionary for the word, it just might be in there.
17. Peruse your file cabinet with all those files I said to put in there. Now, you know how important those files are and how you need a good filing system.
18. Peruse your note boards and now you know how important your note boards are.
19. Peruse your whole environment, and you certainly know how important your environment is.
20. Move things around in your environment, muscle them.

21. Dust things off. Knocking the dust off and clean things in your environment.
22. Get good sleep.
23. Put what you wrote down next to your bed to remind you of what you are trying to remember.
24. Take breaks from trying to remember it.
25. Relax!
26. Write down the next word or symbol that seems like it can help. Don't shortcut this step and these steps.
27. Write down words that are similar to the words you already wrote down.
28. Get up every morning and look at these words and symbols that are mnemonics to the real thing you're trying to figure out.
29. Physically try to sound out words that are close to what you are trying to remember and write down on a piece of paper what the sounds are like.
30. Look at these things written down every morning.
31. You will gradually get out of the fog this way.
32. Look at websites on your computer that sell things. Try to find products that would remind you of what you're trying to remember.

THE STRUCTURE OF PERSEVERANCE!

33. Write down on paper what products that glow to you to remember what you forgot.
34. Go to the library and try to find a book that has what you forgot in it.
35. Write down the name of the books that might have in them what you forgot.
36. Look at your 180-year calendar.
37. Like a reflex, use pretend-zees and go around and pick up things. Look under what you picked up and try to visualize; what you forgot is underneath, what you picked up.
38. Write down on paper what you see underneath, what you picked up.
39. This list should give you structure to remembering things, so now expand on this list. You should be able to, with a list like this. Exercise this list so you can build confidence on it, so it works. Once it works, you will have the confidence in this list. Do you see how being organized gives you a powerful memory?

*Note: If you interfere with missions, operations, or objectives of a person, you are interfering with the functions of a country, and it is an act of war.

Let's discuss umbrella words! The word *corruption* is an umbrella word! If you are accused of corruption, you are accused of breaking the law. The word *corruption,* in terms of breaking the law, has so many laws that you could have broken pertaining to it. You could have accepted bribery. You could have worked with somebody else in your force and had somebody arrested for a crime—you are corrupt. You make deals with a foreign country; you are corrupt. They explain that if you steal something for a foreign country, you are corrupt. You interfered with an election, you are corrupt to get your side to win. You make deals with your lobbyists, you are corrupt. You lie under oath, you are corrupt. Umbrella words confuse people. They create a fog. You have got to stay focused. Identify umbrella words.

I am a civilian, a federal civilian, and I still carry a pen and notebook everywhere I go. It gives you precision, it gives you perseverance, it makes you efficient, it gives you good memory, and it gives you many things. People who make fun of your character are what? They try to control your every move. There are people out there who have serious control problems. They will try to use humiliation, fear, and your emotions and feelings. They will try to claim you're some type of evil person. They will try to claim you are too square. They will try to claim you're a nerd like, that is something evil. They will try to claim you're insane. They will claim you have a mental illness. They will claim there is something wrong with you. They will try to bully you. They will try to humiliate you on social media. They will attack your identity, your ego, and your superego. They will talk behind your back. Does that make you so paranoid, that you stop being squared away? What type of person are they in your community, a negative or a positive one? Are they beneficial to the community? What type of culture are they trying to develop and why? You want to surround yourself with what type of people? You want to surround yourself with a wide variety of people. And with what skills will they give you? The people whom you surround yourself with should be what type of people? If you cannot figure out your environment, you are in trouble. Start with reading the dictionary. Is that a part of your environment? Is that positive? I give you tools in this book to surround yourself with. Do you want to fail at that? Then what type of person are you? What is your identity? What is your ego? What is your superego? Get a book that is written on Sigmund Freud's theories of identity, ego, and superego. I previously wrote in this book that our military gets intelligence on the enemy based on their zodiac sign. They use the enemy's zodiac sign against them. Would it be smart to buy books on your zodiac signs and see how they can be used against you? Yes, it would; this is a part of figuring out your environment.

During your seven-day test, would it be beneficial to figure out how your environment has conditioned you into thinking? This is also why you need the 180-year calendar. This is why you need all these objects that are mnemonics around you, to figure out your past. What is it that you need to figure out about your past, how you were shaped, sculpted, and conditioned into thinking? Right! How important do you think it is now to figure out your past? What is the 180-year calendar? What does the 180-year calendar do?

CHAPTER 6

Let's discuss the 180-year calendar. This tool is so significant and so powerful it's not even funny. This is a mother lode. Take in these in steps. Read this paragraph in steps. For the 180-year calendar, you make the calendar. It's better if it's the whole year, and all the twelve months are on a single piece of paper. You could this on the computer with a program in one go. You will have 180 pieces of paper with one full year on each paper. One piece of paper will have all twelve months in a full year on one paper. You start it on the year that is ten years before your date of birth. So you will have ten pieces of paper—a piece of paper for each year of the ten years before your date of birth, and then you will have 170 pieces of paper with each piece of paper having a full year of all the twelve months on one piece of paper, for each of the 170 years in your future.

You look at each piece of paper for all 180 years. Look at each date and day to organize your thoughts. Look at the day you were born on the 180 pages of the 180 years. Isolate a time frame of things. Start by looking at your date of birth and then each birthday date for each year after that. Make sure you look at the day your birthday was on. Now you do the same thing for each holiday. Start to imagine what happened on each birthday of your life by looking at the 180-year calendar list. You have all 180 years it takes to do this. Notice the leap years. Try to figure out the day you started school and the day that your school year ended. This totally works! Don't be afraid to do this. While you do this, say to yourself "Never forget what makes you."

Isolate the days and dates that are significant to the things that happened to you. This is a timeline of your life. Before I explain other things, trying to project what is going to happen in your future. You have 170 years after your date of birth on all calendars of one year for each piece of paper. Depending on how old you are in the 180 years of the calendars, that is how many years you have on a timeline for your future. Now can you make future plans? Now, use each date and day on the calendar as a mnemonic, to open up the chapter of each day on what happened on that day. You will have a good memory if you use the process of how to remember "the memory process list" with the 180-year calendar list. Think about how smart you will get by doing this. It's a gradual process, you won't remember everything in one day. Keep this 180-year calendar list forever, and you will remember things that you never remembered before. Think about the vocabulary that you know with this system.

Try that with this system, try to remember the vocabulary you have learned in the past. Every time you hear a word, break down the syllables and figure out the definition of each syllable. You will get a stronger vocabulary by doing this. Try to mentally make a timeline of your life in the order of when things happened. Write it down on paper also. Get those brain muscles pumping. Okay, you must do this also. Take all 180 years of calendars and tape them on a wall or a couple of walls close together. Tape up the 180 calendars in order on the wall. That wall will feel powerful to you. You will feel pressure off that wall. It will be an emotional thing for about seven days.

"It's the wall of life!" You need a lot of notebooks because you will write things down in notebooks—things that you remember from your past. Use the "the memory process list." List things from this wall of calendars. Think about newspapers and the date and day of the newspaper on the front page. This book that I'm writing is about taking a person who doesn't think they are smart and turning them into an intelligent human being.

This next tool coordinates with the 180-year calendar. You have got to do this tool and the 180-year calendar, so you have got to do both of these tools. Don't shortcut things. You want to be solid. This tool is similar to the 180-year calendar tool, but it has a different effect. The more angles you have toward remembering your past the better. This tool fills in a different angle to your past. It's good to use different angles on your memory because you have a pyramid of knowledge. You have a tree of knowledge, so you use different angles on that tree and on that pyramid. The combination of this tool and the 180-year calendar tool is extremely powerful. Use the memory process list on this tool also. You can use the memory process list" for everything in this book and everything in your life.

The tool that you use in correlation to the 180-year calendar is a "notebook of life." That is what you write in the notebook. You physically write in the notebook starting with the year, before you were born, the date and day, in your own writing. The first line in the notebook will be January 1, and the year is the year before your birthday. Write the subsequent dates, and after that, on the lines after that date. When you get to the date of birth, you start to concentrate on what your surroundings would have been as far as what might have been in the news. Don't forget

THE STRUCTURE OF PERSEVERANCE!

about the leap years. The leap years will mess up if you write in the wrong date on a leap year. Focus on what date you would have met people. Focus on what day that was on. Focus on the day that holidays are on. Focus on things that you already remember and match the dates when that could have happened.

*Note: You have got to actively use this book: you have got to have it in your active memory. You have got to apply this book to every dimension and realm that you are active in.

*Note: While doing and going deep in thought with the 180-year calendar, "The Wall of Life!" and "The Notebook of Life," you isolate and identify the things in your life that you run into, that coordinate with the "Where you are at and what you are in" list. Identify which is psychological warfare and which is political warfare.

You might not think this has nothing to do with perseverance, but it does need you to be a mentally strong person to have perseverance! It is extremely important, how you visualize yourself. You have got to go "above and beyond" in visualizing yourself:

1. Visualize yourself as a writer.
2. Visualize yourself as speaker.
3. Visualize yourself as the president of a media channel.

4. Visualize yourself as a general.
5. Visualize yourself as a medical doctor.
6. Visual yourself as a professor.
7. Visualize yourself as a lawyer.
8. Visualize yourself as a physics professor.
9. Visualize yourself as a spatial epidemiologist.
10. Visualize yourself as an economist.
11. Visualize yourself working in a file room.
12. Visualize yourself as a coach.
13. Visualize yourself as a leader in your community.
14. Visualize yourself doing surgical strikes.
15. Visualize divide and conquer.
16. Visualize yourself as nothing but with a 4.0 GPA.
17. Visualize yourself with nothing but 100 percent in all your classes and grades.
18. Visualize yourself as 100 percent piercing the enemy.
19. Visualize yourself as 100 percent puncturing the enemy.
20. Visualize yourself as nothing but 100 percent penetration.
21. Visualize yourself as a general; put on your thinking cap, a general's hat.
22. Visualize yourself as Big Red 1.

THE STRUCTURE OF PERSEVERANCE!

You need to practice. Assimilate things. Assimilate you're being a speaker and make speeches. Make different kinds of speeches. Read a book on how to make a speech. Work on your weaknesses. Practice giving speeches by pretending you are talking to a tree.

Mental obstacles are either psychological warfare or political warfare. An example of political warfare is body language. The body language that you are surrounded with is extremely important. It can funnel you in a direction that you are not aware of. Mind reading. Everyone mind reads from the body language of other persons. You do this instantaneously as you're in contact with another person. You learn body language at a very early age from the day you were born. Did you make your decision on what the person is thinking from their body language with free will or was it determinism? Remembering body language is harder. There are ways to write it down, but maybe not every detail. How did you get funneled into thinking that was the way that person was thinking? How did you get vacuumed into thinking that is how that person was thinking? The semantics of body language were implying that you should think this way But should you think that way? Remember the full semantics that they are communicating to you with; it can be a result of the impact of determinism on them. What is the substantive evidence that that was the way or that person was thinking? What culture do they come from? Are you inferring this political picture correctly? What culture do you come from that you used to infer this decision on what they are thinking? Determinism is the environmental forces around that forced you to think that this is the way to do it, think it. You did not come up with these conclusions with free will. Determinism means you did not come up with the conclusion with a free will. Determinism is you conducted these actions as a result from your environment, and you had no choice but to do it that way; you did not do it because of free will. Did you buy that product under free will or was it determinism? Determinism is you getting funneled into buying that product; it was not free will. But what's in your environment that got you to buy this product? Business marketers get taught on how to funnel people into buying the product. If you actively use this book, it will break down the way you get funneled. What do the business marketers do to funnel you into buying this product? How did they condition you into thinking you should buy the product? How did they shape you and sculpt you into thinking you should buy this product? What conformity tactics did they use to get you to think you should buy this product? Are you a leader or a follower?

What makes a leader? Leaders have structure. What is their structure? A leader is somebody who has perseverance, and you are reading *The Structure of Perseverance*. What type of leader are you? You lead by example, but is your example a bad example? Are you a leader who makes decisions with determinism or free will? Are you a partisan leader or a nonpartisan leader? Do you back the vacuum and are a part of the vacuum, or are you a leader? Picking up on the tactics being used on you will help you be a leader. It's extremely critical that you know what the perspective of yourself is. Determinism is a decision that was made from this sequence: this is what happened, so that is what happened, and this is what must happen.

If you're a lawyer and you prove your client broke the law because of determinism, what does that mean? That is how important figuring out determinism is. What semantics are getting you to make that decision? Body language is extremely important when you inspect the angles and premises in the morale category of the "Where you are at and what you are in" list. The obstacle course of psychological warfare and political warfare never stops. What are you going to do to be on top of it?

Determinism can be a result of the opposite gender. You saw a commercial with an alluring person who gave you some warm thoughts, and a year later you bought the product. What subliminal message did they use to capture your thoughts? They made a commercial with a grandma who looks like yours or reminds you of yours, so you bought the product. The word *love* is a bottomless-pit word. How about a commercial where they make the product super large, maybe larger than you—is that a tactic? They make a commercial that makes you cry. They make a commercial that gets you to think this is cute. They make the commercial that claims their product is the number 1 product. The symbol of 1 is beyond powerful. Wear a hat that has nothing on it, but with the symbol 1, you will feel how powerful that symbol is. What is the determinism behind the symbol of 1? They make a commercial that makes your mouth water. You have got to match these tactics with the categories in the "Where you are at and what are you in" list. Rumors create a determinism. How dangerous are rumors? Look around you and figure out what's around you; who is controlled by rumors? Why can't people say as a reflex to every statement made around them "That is a rumor"?

What develops from a myth? Millions of rumors. We are surrounded by nothing but rumors. Are you

THE STRUCTURE OF PERSEVERANCE!

a part of that vacuum? Are you the funnel, or are you what is getting funneled? Do you make funnels and vacuums, or has the funnel or vacuum put you into submission and you are a part of the crowd in which determinism took control of you? Are you getting converted into something else? What is that that is converting you? Everybody has weaknesses. If you have a weakness where something stops you from completing your missions, operations, or objectives, you have got to work on that weakness to make you stronger in that area, so nothing in that area stops you from completing your missions, operations, and objectives. What are the devices and control devices that are funneling you?

Leverage is a device. Do people have a leverage that they are using on you? A leverage is usually extremely powerful. A Leverage can be, if you don't do this, then this is what will happen. Salesmen use this tool. When you buy a new car and if you buy the cheaper car, this is what will happen. Each one of the thirty categories in the "Where you are at and what are you in" list can be a leverage device. How can we use these leverage devices on other people? This is when you become the professor. You are the director of the movie, you control the rumors, you make the rumors in your community. Like I said, wear a hat with the number 1 symbol on it to get everybody to think you're number 1. Walk around with a briefcase that is handcuffed to your hand. People will think you are carrying something important. This means you're an important person. Your charisma is what? You go to bars and you drink the number 1 beer or drink the number 1 drink. Do you want that to be your charisma? You outdrink everybody on the block; do you want that charisma? That is the charisma that will come back to haunt you. You want a positive charisma. Let me describe an ecosystem.

A magnet has an ecosystem. The ecosystem of a magnet is the magnetic field around the magnet. You can say that uranium has an ecosystem around it—the radiation around the uranium is the ecosystem. You can say the planet Earth has a north pole and a south pole in which the planet Earth is like a magnet. The earth is magnetic, so the planet earth has an ecosystem. For the moon that rotates around the planet Earth, the moon is magnetic and also has an ecosystem. You can say, by that observation, that the moon's magnetic field affects the planet Earth's magnetic field because magnets affect other magnets. You can say that the moon does affect the ecosystem on the planet Earth. So the moon does affect the Earth's weather.

THE STRUCTURE OF PERSEVERANCE!

With that said, what is global warming? It is the changing of the weather, right? Why does the weather change? Well, you can say the weather does change because of the moon having a magnetic effect on the planet Earth; it affects the planet Earth's ecosystem. Do the planet Earth and the moon rotate around the sun? Yes, both of them rotate around the sun. Does the sun have a magnetic field? Does the sun have an ecosystem? Yes, it does! Does the planet Earth and the moon travel around the sun on the exact same path every year—no, it does not! The planet Earth and the moon do not travel on the exact same path around the sun; it constantly changes. The moon does not travel around the planet Earth on the same path. The planet Earth itself wobbles on its axis; it doesn't spin circularly without wobbling. Do all the other planets have a magnetic field? Yes, they do! All the other planets have an ecosystem.

Do the other planets affect the planet Earth's weather? Yes, they do. So who is controlling the weather? It should be safe to say that the whole solar system is controlling that planet Earth's weather. Who invented this idea that there is global warming changing the planet Earth's weather? Was it the weather people on your news channels? Who thinks they can control the weather? How are you going to change the weather to where the snow does not melt on the North Pole? You can't! Everything has an ecosystem. Vehicles on the road have an ecosystem. Your house has an ecosystem. The roof on your house has an ecosystem. Your roof gives off radiant energy, that is an ecosystem. Plastic has an ecosystem. Finally, I must say all material has an ecosystem. Let me see you eliminate all material. You should have an idea of ecosystems now.

Charisma is like an ecosystem, try to think of it that way. Okay, flowers have charisma. One type of flower means love, another type of flower means a sign of health, another flower means you're caring. So objects have charisma. Yes, they do. What kind of charisma do you have? Well, if you wear a flower, that means you're caring, then you have the charisma of being caring, An army tank means the total destruction symbol. What is the cause and effect of the total destruction symbol? If you wear a flower, that means caring; what is the cause and effect of that? When thinking about determinism, you have got to think about cause and effect. What is the cause and effect of the names of the businesses around you? What if you named a business Calculations? What effect would that have on your community? What if you named a business Graphs? What effect would that have on your community?

THE STRUCTURE OF PERSEVERANCE!

What if you name a business Computations? What effect would that have on your community? What if you name a business Caution? What effect would it have on the community? What if you named a business Safety? What effect would that have on the community? Objects have charisma. What if you named a business Solutions? What effect would that have on the community? What if you named a business Solve Puzzles? What effect would that have on the community?

Let's think of some other positive names that might be a little bit harder to figure out. What if you named a business Notebook? What effect would that have on the community? What if you named a business Depth? What effect would it have on the community? What if you named a business Morale? What effect would it have on the community? What if you named a business Perseverance? What effect would it have on the community? What if you named a business Statistics? What effect would that have on the community. What if you named a business Dictionary? What effect would it have on the community?

Do you see how important signs are now? Can you imagine driving down a street like that? What would you be thinking at the end of that street? Okay, so if I say you drive down a street and forget what your grocery list is, what kind of street is that? Is that a detrimental street? Every street you drive down is an obstacle course. Every street you drive down has equations. What are the equations of the streets you drive down? Your eyes are that sensitive. Let's think of one sign on the street that is a name of a business that has a very negative name. What if you name a business a very negative name like Forget? How about that name? What effect would that have on the community? What is the premise of these names on the businesses? The word *premises*—what are the names of these businesses implying? How can names of businesses affect you? Signs are extremely important. What is the cause and effect to the names of the businesses? How focused are you? Can you remember when you drove down a street as an obstacle course? Will you actually apply that when you drive? Here is an example: if you own both a cat and a dog, the cat acts like the dog and the dog acts like the cat. People are the same way. If you are friends with a cat, you will act like at cat. If you are friends with a dog, you act like a dog. Choose your friends wisely. Conformity! What causes you to desire something? How many other people desire that same object for the same reason? Determinism is that something that has affected you in which you are following through with it because of motionless martial arts or a butterfly effect that has affected you to do those motions. The things that you are doing is determinism because you're not doing them with a free will.

I'm going to simplify the meanings of identity, ego, and superego so you can understand them better. I will explain these better after I present the main definitions first. These are my definitions:

1. Identity is what your identity is; it is also what your overall charisma is.
2. Ego is how confident you are in doing things.
3. Superego has identity and ego in it but includes your emotional side and your feeling side.

When somebody attacks your identity; they are attacking your title. They try to say your title is not what it is. They shape your title into meaning something else. They use cartoon spoofs. They use words to reshape your title. They use pictures to reshape your title. They use devices to attack what your overall charisma is. They attack what your charisma is with words and devices. They attack you to shut you down. They attack you to stop you.

When somebody attacks your ego, they attack the identity of your ego. They attack what your ego is believed to be on a public level, the way the public identifies your ego to be. It will feel like it's true because they use the history of how you did things. It's not your real ego, or is it? You need a high ego. It's good to have a high ego. If people did not have high egos, then we wouldn't have lawyers and doctors. You wouldn't have leaders! They use cartoon spoofs. They use words! They attack you to shut you down. They attack you to stop you.

When people attack your superego, it's dangerous because it feels like they are boxing you in. They step on your identity. They step on your ego. They step on your feelings. They step on your emotions. They use cartoon spoofs. They use words. They use devices to attack you in a way that goes to your heart. They attack you to shut you down. They attack you to stop you.

Now I will tell you about the tactic that the enemy uses also to shut you down, a tool they use to stop you. They do filibusters to convince you with statements like "You don't even know how to tie your shoes yet," and they have all kinds of angles for that. The reflex is usually a self-inspection of yourself. A tool I would like to add to this to counter it is "If you don't have an answer, make up an answer!" How do you do that? Maybe the first thing you should think of is that bowl on your shelf with the

THE STRUCTURE OF PERSEVERANCE!

cans of soup in it with the message of making something with the dictionary, with your Library, with your "Wall of Life," with your "Notebook of Life," and so on.

Now I'm going to give you examples of tactics that are literally used on me. It's military-related, but it should expand the views for yourself.

Even if you are not military, you may sit down to get something to eat at a restaurant. The person next to you asks you, "Are you or were military?" You say, "Yes, I was military!" That person will say, "Yeah, I was in the military and I didn't learn a thing!" He is trying to get you to forget everything you learned in the military by saying he was in the military and he didn't learn anything.

You meet somebody walking. They bump into you and say, "Hi, were you in the military?" I say, "Yes!" He says, "I was too. I was a pilot on the F-15!" You say, "That sounds like a neat job!" He says, "I couldn't handle what I did as a pilot. I want to forget it all and I did." He wants you to forget what you learned in the military.

Another person comes up to you and says, "Hi, were you in the military?" I say, "Yes, I was in the military." He says, "Me too, I was in the military and I'm a nobody." He or she is trying to get you to think that you are a nobody.

Somebody will come up to you and say, "Hi, were you in the military?" I say, "Yes, I was in the military." They will say, "I was in the military, and they taught me nothing!" They want to think you know nothing. These people even, if they were military, are the enemy of the country, and there are laws to back that. They are trying to get you to forget what you learned in the military! They want you to forget who you are. Never forget what makes you, you! When you get out, you are a federal citizen. The property you own in a way is federal property. If people attack you, they are attacking the country and it's an act of war. The way I see it, they never got out of the military, just like they tell you "Once you're in the military, you are always in the military!" Right now, the law doesn't see it that way, and there are going to be changes with that on how you arrest someone who is former military.

CHAPTER 7

Inferring, interpreting, and identifying—I am about to give you three tools for inferring, interpretating, and identifying to practice with.

The first tool is the Stroop test. What you do is get a piece of blank white paper, then you get a red marker, then with the red marker you write real big on the white piece of paper the word BLUE. Look at the paper. It should look like this:

BLUE

Follow the directions above, that word above should be in red.

Now get somebody to do this too. Hold up the paper to the person so they can see it, then ask them "What color is the ink?" If they get it wrong, they would have said, "The color of the ink is *blue*!" That is the wrong answer. The right answer is the word is written in *red.*

How observant are you? If you get this wrong, it does not mean you're not observant. This is only a test to make you aware of that type of situation.

Okay, the second tool for inferring, interpretating, and identifying is the Wasson confirmation bias. What is the Wasson confirmation bias? Well, I'm going to explain it the way I'm going to explain it.

1. First you have a full deck of cards.
2. There are two suits in the card deck that are red and two suits of cards in the card deck that are black.
3. The dealer puts four cards face down, so you can't see the face of the cards. The dealer turns over three cards showing the face of the cards. The dealer makes sure the cards of all three cards that are facing up are the black suits.
4. The dealer says, "This fourth card should be red!"
5. The dealer turns the card over, and it's red.
6. You repeat this process again. It's different this time.
7. First you have a full deck of cards.
8. There are two suits in the card deck that are red and two suits in the card deck that are black.

THE STRUCTURE OF PERSEVERANCE!

9. The dealer puts four cards face down, so you can't see the face of the cards. The dealer turns over three cards showing the face of the cards. The dealer this time makes sure this time that the three cards facing up are all red suits.
10. The dealer says, "The fourth card should be black!"
11. The dealer turns over the card, and it is black.
12. You repeat this process again; it's different this time.
13. First you have a full deck of cards.
14. There are two suits in the card deck that are red and there are two suits in the card deck that are black.
15. The dealer puts four cards face down, so you can't see the face of the cards. The dealer turns over three cards showing the face of the cards. The dealer this time makes sure all three cards facing up are black suits.
16. This time the dealer says, "The fourth card is going to be black!"
17. There is a third person who asks you, "What is the fourth card going to be?"

So what bias are you going to have? What bias are you picking? The two previous times it was the opposite color. What is your prediction? Are you biased that it will not be the opposite color, or are you biased that it will be the same color? That's confusing because bias means you don't like something.

For the third tool to inferring, interpretating, and identifying, you have got to do on your own. I did it in the second grade. Study optical illusions. You don't really have to do that.

*Note: You have the framework. Are you going to consciously use and apply the tools in this book? That is the question.

The psychological warfare and political warfare angle and premise that a powerful figure gets an office, visits with you, and claims that they want to close your file is a powerful move, especially if they have leverage on you also. Your response should be "No, all my files stay open." Anyone who makes a comment about how they want to close your book should be ignored. All your books should stay open. If you leave books open where you live, this gives you charisma. You can access those books easy with your memory. If the book is closed, it's an action of you dosing your book, that you need to remember what's in it. It feels good when you leave the dictionary open.

THE STRUCTURE OF PERSEVERANCE!

Everyone is sensitive to their surroundings, even the tough guys. You want to build skills of thinking outside the box, like staring down on a globe—you are on the outside looking in. This is when you discover a lot of things about a lot of situations. Say you set up an obstacle course of obstacles. You have five offices you have got to go into, and the five different offices can be set up like an equation!. The way you figure out what is in the offices that affected you with psychological warfare and political warfare is you do a seven-day test after each office visit that you went into. For the seven-day test, you think outside the box. Lock yourself in the box to think outside the box. It's good to say out loud "I'm locking myself in." What was in this office? What kind of objects? What was said in the office? How did the people use what was in the office to funnel you in a new direction? Is the new direction a decoy direction? Did they force you to say anything? Write down what was in the office. Break it down. Divide and conquer.

Look down at what you wrote, then focus on a faraway star. Focus on that letter in the mail. Is the television in the office you're trying to inspect? Is social media in the office you're trying to inspect? Yes, the television and social media are in this office. That is an obstacle. You have got to identify obstacles and list them in the thirty categories I gave you in the list "Where you are at and what are you in" list. You isolate and identify the obstacles or targets and put them in a category of the "Where you are at and what are you in" list. This motion of putting things in that list is what helps you overcome the obstacle, obstacles, the maze of obstacles, the puzzle of obstacles, or the algorithm of obstacles.

The obstacles can be psychological warfare or political warfare. Psychological warfare is words. Political warfare is objects. You can have a maze, a puzzle, an algorithm of words, which is psychological warfare, or you can have a maze, puzzle, or an algorithm of objects. It is what was orchestrated, like music. Music is orchestrated. A movie is orchestrated. A war is orchestrated. The military has algorithms of psychological warfare and political warfare on the enemy. The military has an orchestra that plays during wars, just like in the old movies. There is a drummer and a bugler out in front of the formation when they attack the enemy, or the orchestra can be behind the military while they attack the enemy. The soldiers move to the beat of the drums. The algorithm is a maze, a puzzle, and corrugated like an orchestra of music. A movie is a blend of words and objects producing an outcome. What is the cause and effect of the words and objects in a movie? What is the algorithm of the maze and puzzle of a movie? It's a movie, it's made up of words and objects in an algorithm, an orchestrated algorithm. A movie is an orchestrated algorithm of psychological warfare, which is words, and political warfare, which is objects. It has both, that is why it's so powerful.

Social media has both, that is why it's so powerful. A commercial has both. A bulletin board has both. A billboard has both. Colors in an orchestrated algorithm are extremely powerful, especially if only the eight colors of a prism are used. The prism is a triangle the shape of nature. The triangle is the strongest and most powerful structure. A premise should always have three things in it. Always look for the triangle. Identify the triangle of information. The information can be words or it can be objects. Words can be in a triangle and objects can be in a triangle. This is also why movies are so powerful and social media is so powerful. They are triangular. A premise is triangular. I am going to give you an example with a premise right now. The premise does have objects in it. A word can describe an object. When you think of a word that is an object, you think of an object. If I say tree, which is an object, what object do you think of? Do you think maple tree or an oak tree or a redwood tree. Objects have semantics and charisma. A rock has semantics and charisma. The Tiger's Eye mineral or rock in your environment is supposed to do many things, like make you feel mentally strong.

Okay, now I will give you the structure of a premise that has three things in it for sure, like a triangle. It has three angles and premises in it. Each sentence is an angle and premise. You can have a triangle in a triangle:

1. Everyone in the city speaks Italian.
2. Stan is from the city.
3. Therefore, Stan speaks Italian.

The first angle and premise has three things in it—one is everyone, two is city, and three is Italian. The second angle and premise has three things in it; one is Stan, two is from, and three is city. The third angle and premise has three things in it; one is Stan, two is speaks, and three is Italian. Each angle and premise has three things in it, and all three sentences are angles and premises.

The overall premise is a sentence: sentence one, sentence two, and sentence three. This is what I'll call a full premise. If you combine angle and premise 1, the first sentence, and angle and premise 2, the second sentence, you get a third angle and premise:

THE STRUCTURE OF PERSEVERANCE!

sentence three, the conclusion. Sentence 3 or angle and premise 3 is the conclusion of angle and premise of one and two put together.

*Note: A premise with a conclusion is powerful because it is based on facts. Lawyers will try to prove that there is an error in the facts.

*Note: A premise with a conclusion hypnotizes us, mesmerizes us, conditions us, conforms us. It creates determinism, it funnels us, it creates vacuums, it creates a butterfly effects, it cultivates us, it controls us, etc.

Okay, now let's get back to movies, social media, commercials, bulletin boards, and billboards. They use feelings and emotions to captivate your attention, capture your attention. It stops your mission, your operations, and objectives. They also sculpt who you are. These emotions and feelings are what you have become. They are determinism, not free will. These movies, social media, commercials, bulletin boards, and billboards are the cause of what effects your identity, ego, and superego. The movies, social media, commercials, bulletin boards, and billboards change your identity, ego, and superego into what? Combine the colors and emotions and feelings you're exposed too from these premises of movies, social media, commercials, bulletin boards, and billboards, and then you become what? That combination on you is deadly.

The people making these movies, social media, commercials, bulletin boards, and billboards use feelings and emotions to control you. Music gives you feelings and emotions, that is why that is so powerful. It's universal meaning affects all. And the all is us, and we are all, that is why we all act the same way. Maybe we should look at a list of feelings and emotions to see how they captivate us cultivate us. The people who make movies, social media, commercials, bulletin boards, and billboards know what they are doing, or they even do it by instinct to use our feelings and emotions to control us, cultivate us. This is why we need to take such a good look at a list of feelings and emotions. Every feeling and emotion is an angle and premise to stop our missions, operations, and objectives. They use feelings and emotions to stop us from completing our missions, operations, and objectives. We should be really interested in this list because it breaks it down into the angles and premises used. Your friends and family are a constant movie. Each word in the "initial list" is defined as what reactions you have to these feelings and emotions. It's description of how you feel or the emotion you have is in the "secondary list." Each word in this "initial list" are control devices. These next two lists are actually the same list. Each one of these words in this list can be used as leverage on us. Each word can be a leverage device in this list. The next two lists, the "initial list" and the "secondary list" are the exact same list. *I'm listing these full lists because they are that important.*

*Note: Identify how they got you to have this emotion and feeling or emotions and feelings.

Okay. Here is first initial list:

1. *Death* is an explosion of feelings and emotions, but how is death being used on us?
2. *Faith* is something you have feelings and emotions for.
3. *Love* is also extremely powerful, you have both feelings and emotions with love.
4. *Afraid*
5. *Angry*
6. *Courage*
7. *Disconnect*
8. *Dislike*
9. *Embarrassment*
10. *Energy*
11. *Gratefulness*
12. *Helplessness*
13. *Hopefulness*
14. *Hurt*

15. *Insecurity*
16. *Introspectiveness*
17. *Joyfulness*
18. *Kindness*
19. *Love*
20. *Sadness*
21. *Surprised*
22. *Unkindness*

This next list is the "secondary list" as described before at the end of the last paragraph. I am going to break this list down even further because it's that important. This next list explains how each emotion and feeling makes you feel as described in the definitions of the word in bold in the next list. They know how you will respond if they successfully make you feel a certain way in the initial list and what your emotions and feelings will be by them making you feel that way.

1. *Death*
   A. All emotions
   B. All feelings

2. *Faith*
   A. All emotions
   B. All feelings

THE STRUCTURE OF PERSEVERANCE!

3. *Love*
   A. All emotions
   B. All feelings.

4. *Afraid*
   A. Agitated
   B. Alarmed
   C. Antsy
   D. Anxious
   E. Apprehensive
   F. Cautious
   G. Concerned
   H. Cowardly
   I. Distressed
   J. Dread
   K. Edgy
   L. Fearful
   M. Foreboding
   N. Frazzled
   O. Fretful
   P. Frightened
   Q. Guarded
   R. Hesitant
   S. Horrified
   T. Hysterical
   U. Jumpy
   V. Nervous

W. Panic
X. Paralyzed
Y. Paranoid
Z. Petrified
AA. Restless
BB. Scared
CC. Shaken
DD. Skeptical
EE. Startled
FF. Stressed
GG. Tense
HH. Terrified
II. Timid
JJ. Trepidation
KK. Twitchy
LL. Uptight
MM. Vigilant
NN. Wary
AA. Worried

5. *Angry*
   A. Aggravated
   B. Animosity
   C. Annoyed
   D. Antagonistic
   E. Antipathy
   F. Bitter

THE STRUCTURE OF PERSEVERANCE!

G. Bothered
H. Burning
I. Choleric
J. Cold
K. Consternation
L. Contempt
M. Cross
N. Disgruntled
O. Enmity
P. Exasperated
Q. Frustrated
R. Furious
S. Grouchy
T. Harassed
U. Hostile
V. Ill-tempered
W. Impatient
X. Indignant
Y. Irritated
Z. Irate
AA. Irascible
BB. Mad
CC. Miffed
DD. Moody
EE. Nasty
FF. Offended
GG. Outraged

HH. Peevish
II. Perturbed
JJ. Livid
KK. Resentful
LL. Petulant
MM. Rage
NN. Rattled
OO. Resentment
PP. Shaking
QQ. Sour
RR. Testy
SS. Tetchy
TT. Vexed
UU. Vindictive
VV. Wrathful

6. *Courageous*
    A. Adventurous
    B. Audacious
    C. Bold
    D. Brave
    E. Capable
    F. Certain
    G. Cocky
    H. Confident
    I. Comfortable
    J. Daring

THE STRUCTURE OF PERSEVERANCE!

  K. Determined
  L. Fearless
  M. Free
  N. Grounded
  O. Gutsy
  P. Powerful
  Q. Proud
  R. Resolute
  S. Strong
  T. Superior
  U. Tenacious
  V. Tough
  W. Valiant
  X. Vehement
  Y. Worthy

7. *Disconnected*
  A. Adrift
  B. Alienated
  C. Alone
  D. Aloof
  E. Bored
  F. Conflicted
  G. Consternated
  H. Cranky
  I. Denial
  J. Detached

K. Disillusioned
L. Disinterested
M. Distant
N. Distracted
O. Empty
P. Fatigued
Q. Groggy
R. Hollow
S. Jaded
T. Indifferent
U. Isolated
V. Lethargic
W. Listless
X. Lost
Y. Neutral
Z. Numb
AA. Powerless
BB. Preoccupied
CC. Puzzled
DD. Reluctance
EE. Removed
FF. Resignation
GG. Resistance
HH. Sheepish
II. Shut Down
JJ. Sluggish
KK. Sullen

THE STRUCTURE OF PERSEVERANCE!

    LL. Torn
    MM. Uneasy
    NN. Withdrawn

8. *Dislike*
   A. Abhorrence
   B. Aversion
   C. Detest
   D. Disdain
   E. Disgust
   F. Envious
   G. Grudging
   H. Hate
   I. Repugnance
   J. Revolted
   K. Scorn

9. *Embarrassed*
   A. Appalled
   B. Apologetic
   C. Ashamed
   D. Chagrined
   E. Compunction
   F. Contrite
   G. Flustered
   H. Foolish
   I. Guilty

J. Humbled
K. Humored
L. Inferior
M. Inhibited
N. Mortified
O. Pathetic
P. Regretful
Q. Repentant
R. Shame
S. Self-conscious
T. Sorry
U. Submissive
V. Useless
W. Weak
X. Worthless

10. *Energized*
    A. Alert
    B. Alive
    C. Animated
    D. Aroused
    E. Bouncy
    F. Curious
    G. Fanatical
    H. Fascinated
    I. Feisty
    J. Fervor

THE STRUCTURE OF PERSEVERANCE!

    K. Gung-ho
    L. Gusto
    M. Hyper
    N. Intense
    O. Psyched
    P. Pumped
    Q. Snappy
    R. Sprightly
    S. Thirst
    T. Titillated
    U. Vindicated
    V. Zeal
    W. Zest

11. *Grateful*
    A. Blessed
    B. Fortunate
    C. Gratified
    D. Relish
    E. Savor
    F. Thankful
    G. Touched

12. *Helpless*
    A. Awkward
    B. Baffled
    C. Challenged

D. Clueless
   E. Complacent
   F. Disturbed
   G. Exhausted
   H. Fatigued
   I. Fragile
   J. Impotent
   K. Incapable
   L. Needy
   M. Overwhelmed
   N. Pathetic
   O. Perplexed
   P. Powerless
   Q. Resigned
   R. Sensitive
   S. Trapped
   T. Victim

13. *Hopeful*
    A. Anticipation
    B. Craving
    C. Desiring
    D. Eager
    E. Encouraged
    F. Expectant
    G. Hankering

THE STRUCTURE OF PERSEVERANCE!

    H. Optimistic
    I. Trusting

14. *Hurt*
    A. Agony
    B. Betrayed
    C. Humiliated
    D. Pained
    E. Stung
    F. Suffering
    G. Suffocated
    H. Tormented
    I. Tortured
    J. Traumatized

15. *Insecure*
    A. Bashful
    B. Befuddled
    C. Bewildered
    D. Cynical
    E. Confused
    F. Doubtful
    G. Possessive
    H. Shy
    I. Woozy

16. *Introspective*
    A. Absorbed
    B. Brooding
    C. Contemplative
    D. Engrossed
    E. Enlightened
    F. Inspired
    G. Interested
    H. Meditative
    I. Nostalgic
    J. Pensive
    K. Reflective
    L. Solemn
    M. Stirred
    N. Wonder

17. *Joyful*
    A. Amused
    B. Awed
    C. Bemused
    D. Bliss
    E. Blithe
    F. Bonhomie
    G. Buddy
    H. Buoyant
    I. Carefree
    J. Cheerful

THE STRUCTURE OF PERSEVERANCE!

K. Delectation
L. Delighted
M. Delirious
N. Ebullient
O. Ecstatic
P. Elated
Q. Enchanted
R. Enjoyment
S. Entertained
T. Enthusiastic
U. Euphoric
V. Excited
W. Exhilarated
X. Exuberant
Y. Felicitous
Z. Genial
AA. Giddy
BB. Glad
CC. Gleeful
DD. Goofy
EE. Happy
FF. Humorous
GG. Invigorated
HH. Jocular
II. Jocund
JJ. Jolly
KK. Jovial

LL. Jubilant
MM. Liberated
NN. Lighthearted
OO. Lively
PP. Lucky
QQ. Merry
RR. Mirthful
SS. Mischievous
TT. Motivated
UU. Passionate
VV. Perky
WW. Playful
XX. Pleasure
YY. Positive
ZZ. Proud
AAA. Rapture
BBB. Reassured
CCC. Relieved
DDD. Sanguine
EEE. Satisfied
FFF. Silly
GGG. Sunny
HHH. Thrilled
III. Triumphant
JJJ. Upbeat
KKK. Vibrant

18. *Kind*
    A. Caring
    B. Compassionate
    C. Cordial
    D. Earnest
    E. Empathetic
    F. Pitying
    G. Self-loving
    H. Sincere
    I. Sympathetic
    J. Succor
    K. Tender
    L. Thoughtful
    M. Vulnerable
    N. Warm
    O. Welcoming

19. *Loving*
    A. Accepting
    B. Admiring
    C. Adoring
    D. Adulation
    E. Affectionate
    F. Ardor
    G. Attached
    H. Attracted
    I. Captivated

J. Devoted
K. Enthralled
L. Felicitous
M. Fondness
N. Fulfilled
O. Infatuated
P. Intimate
Q. Intoxicated
R. Present
S. Protective
T. Safe
U. Sensual
V. Warm
W. Worthy
X. Peaceful
Y. Calm
Z. Centered
AA. Collected
BB. Comforted
CC. Composed
DD. Content
EE. Ease
FF. Free
GG. Mellow
HH. Mollified
II. Open
JJ. Pacified

THE STRUCTURE OF PERSEVERANCE!

- KK. Patient
- LL. Phlegmatic
- MM. Receptive
- NN. Relaxed
- OO. Secure
- PP. Settled
- QQ. Sure
- RR. Trusting
- SS. Tranquil

20. *Sadness*
    - A. Aching
    - B. Alienated
    - C. Angst
    - D. Anguish
    - E. Blue
    - F. Choked
    - G. Crestfallen
    - H. Crummy
    - I. Crushed
    - J. Defeated
    - K. Dejected
    - L. Depressed
    - M. Despair
    - N. Despondent
    - O. Devastated
    - P. Disappointed

Q. Discouraged
R. Dismal
S. Doleful
T. Down
U. Downcast
V. Excluded
W. Forlorn
X. Gloomy
Y. Grief
Z. Heartbroken
AA. Homesick
BB. Hopeless
CC. Hurt
DD. Lonely
EE. Longing
FF. Melancholy
GG. Mournful
HH. Pained
II. Pessimistic
JJ. Remorseful
KK. Sick
LL. Somber
MM. Sorrowful
NN. Teary
OO. Troubled
PP. Unhappy
QQ. Upset

THE STRUCTURE OF PERSEVERANCE!

    RR. Weary
    SS. Wistful
    TT. Woe
    UU. Wretched
    VV. Yearning

21. *Surprised*
    A. Amazed
    B. Astonished
    C. Astounded
    D. Breathless
    E. Disbelief
    F. Dubious
    G. Dumbfounded
    H. Flabbergasted
    I. Floored
    J. Quizzical
    K. Scandalized
    L. Serendipitous
    M. Shock
    N. Speechless
    O. Stunned
    P. Stupefied

22. *Unkind*
    A. Crafty
    B. Cruel

C. Derisive
D. Greedy
E. Petty
F. Selfish
G. Smug
H. Berate
I. Vituperative
J. Castigate
K. Immoral

What do these emotions and feelings do to us? Exactly what is in the definition of the word? The people who make movies, social media, commercials, bulletin boards, and billboards can predict what you will do next by using this list. The people who make movies, social media posts, commercials, bulletin boards, and billboards can predict how you will feel after you see what they want you to see. Movies, social media posts, commercials, bulletin boards, and billboards are a blend of things like colors, words, props, or objects of charism, body language, feelings and emotions, mysticism, coincidences, beauty, happiness, death, and many more things to conform you and to cultivate you to do things. Those inputs are determinism.

You wear what you see people wear on television, social media, commercials, bulletin boards—

it's determinism. You talk like what you see on television, social media, commercials, bulletin boards, and billboards—it's determinism. The shutter speed of watching television, social media, and commercials is so fast, but your brain senses all of it in a billionth of a second. This is how I know speed-reading at shutter speed is real. Your eyes are that sensitive. You see commercials over and over, and they condition you to think a certain way. You drive down a street filled with signs, and you feel the emotions and feelings of the signs as you drive. Each one of these emotions and feelings is an angle and premise. They use these emotions and feelings to control you, to stop you from completing your missions, your operations, and your objectives. The media, social media, commercials, bulletin boards, and billboards sucker you in with these emotions and feelings. Because they are powerful on you, they want you to feel what they are saying. They have stories about the underdog. Millions of people love the underdog, so it's the love that gets you.

The movies, social media, commercials, bulletin boards, and billboards give energy, but energy to do what? Control your energy by writing things down. Control your energy by controlling the things you put in your environment. Social media has tools for when you're trying to do a post, and while you are writing the sentence, they give you the next word you are going to write, conforming you into what word they want you to use. Social media gives you tools like 3D pictures and emojis, and you love them; it's the emotions and feelings that get you. They get you to love using the 3D pictures and emojis. Social media is a place where you can express your feelings and emotions, release your emotions, try to impress other people, try to get people to think the way you do. It's such a powerful release that nobody can stop using it long enough to figure out their missions, operations, and objectives. It's so releasing that people forget what their missions, operations, and objectives are. A movie is nothing but a long equation. Break the equation down. Write it down breaking the equation.

Producers of media predict what emotions and feelings you're going to have and how you will react to it. The angles and premises conform and cultivate you into the next emotion and feeling, conforming you to forget you missions, operations, and objectives. It conforms you into a whole another motion. Colors give you emotions and feelings. Yellow makes you feel piercing. Red makes you feel victorious. Blue makes you feel perseverance. Orange makes you feel feared. Brown makes you feel settled down. Green makes you go into deep thought.

THE STRUCTURE OF PERSEVERANCE!

Black makes you aggressive. White makes you feel innocent. They use these colors in a blended equation. Colors shape your environment, your culture. Colors shape your morale. Colors shape your emotions and feelings. A country color code is beyond important. Colors have an impact on you. Words have an impact on you. Objects and props have an impact on you. Colors condition you to think a certain way. Colors conform you. Colors mesmerize you and hypnotize you. What is the equation of colors?

You drive down the road and see a vehicle that is gray; you will feel depressed. What is the equation of colors as you drive down the road? Can you imagine if every color of each vehicle was only the eight colors of the prism? You would have one powerful country. Picture what I'm saying there. Each color that is not one of the eight colors breaks the eight-color code. It sabotages the eight-color code. Each color you see driving down the road conforms you into buying a vehicle, even if it is not one of the colors in the eight-color code. You see a beautiful female in this color of vehicle, so you buy that color. You see a beautiful male in this color of vehicle, so you buy that color. What if it's the color gray? Gray makes you feel depressed. The color teal green mixed with gray makes you feel confused because you don't know what color it is. The determinism of seeing fifty colors and not just the eight colors driving down the road gives you what? Determinism. Yellow gives you the determinism of being piercing. Red gives you the determinism of being victorious. Blue gives you the determinism of perseverance and so on down the whole eight-color list. Bring back our eight-color code of the triangle prism. What you are exposed to while you are awake, you dream about while you are asleep. What are you dreaming about? Fifty different colors. Your dreams are now foggy. What you are exposed to today, you feel tomorrow. Anyway, in the military, they only let you get four hours of sleep at night because the enemy is using psychological and political warfare on you while you're awake. Therefore, you only sleep four hours, so the enemy will not be able to conform you into what the enemy wants to do. You see a misspelled sign, but what you really see is fog. You see a color that is not a part of the eight-color code, and what that does is it make you see? Fog.

You see a color that is not a part of the eight-color code, and it's like seeing a misspelled sign; it creates fog. What if you see a street sign that is violating the eight-color code? It is sabotage to destroy the meaning of the eight colors of the country color code! It is fog and an act of war. Anything that creates fog is an act of war. It is higher than breaking a federal law. Symbols have meanings. The colors in symbols affect you. The colors in objects affect you. What if you went to a college that was named Calculation College? What charisma would that give you? What morale would that give you? What if you went to a college that was named Angry College? What charisma would that give you? What morale would that give you? What if you graduated from a high school called Defiance High School? What charisma would you have? What morale would you have? Let's go through the list of emotions and feelings to show you how they can be used for negotiating with leaders of foreign countries, how they can be used in a detrimental way. What colors, emotions, and feelings were you exposed to before you met with a leader of a foreign country? The determinism before you meet with a leader of a foreign country can be used in a way that cultivates you in the direction the enemy wants you to go in, and how they can control the way you think in a negative way. Your friends and family use the list of emotions and feelings on you like a constant movie.

Here is a list of angles and premises from emotions and feelings that can be used on you in an equation. I will use a couple of words out of the definitions of emotions and feelings to demonstrate how they are used:

1. *Death*—makes you feel like you have come to the end. If you don't come to the end, something will kill you. Heavy losses make you think everything is now at the end of the rope. The color is black.
2. *Faith*—makes you feel like you have got to do something according to faith, which benefits the enemy! The color is white.
3. *Love*—makes you forget your missions, operations, and objectives, for one you are too busy to complete your missions, operations, and objective. You are so in love, nothing else matters. The color is white.
4. *Afraid*—They make you have a fear toward doing your missions, operations, and objectives. They will make you feel *frightened* to stop you from doing your missions, operations, and objectives, by making you afraid to do them. Here is a couple of words that you feel if you are afraid. You feel *distressed* that if you do your missions, operations, and objectives, something bad will happen. You feel *frazzled* and confused about completing your missions, operations, and objectives.

THE STRUCTURE OF PERSEVERANCE!

5. *Angry*—They make you angry, so you don't make controlled decisions. It makes you feel *frustrated* and out of control, they put you off balance. It makes you *impatient*, so you don't make organized, precise decisions. It makes you *moody*, so you base your decisions off of what mood are you in.
6. *Courageous*—You feel like you can do anything. You feel adventurous to do anything, so you might not decide to do the right thing. You feel *fearless* to the point you might attack their strongest force and lose. You feel proud, so *proud*, that you don't listen to the feedback from the people under you. You feel *superior* to the point where you don't think you can make any mistakes, but you end up making a mistake, because you think you are so superior.
7. *Disconnected*—You feel disconnect from your missions, operations, and objectives! You're *bored* of everything, including your missions, operations, and objectives. You feel *denial* that your missions, operations, and objectives will work. You feel so much *fatigue* that you think it's impossible for you to complete your missions, operations, and objectives.

8. *Dislike*—You dislike something so much, even though it's the right decision, that you don't do the right decision. You *detest* something so much it breaks your concentration. You are grudging to the point you only go after the target and forget about your missions, operations, and objectives. You have so much hate you no longer think rational!
9. *Embarrassed*—You are so embarrassed that you won't do your missions, operations, and objectives because if you do them, you will feel embarrassed. You feel so *contrite* that what you feel *contrite* toward is controlling you. You feel *guilty* that you're hurting something, and you don't do your missions, operations, and objectives. You feel *pathetic*, so *pathetic* that you think you're not doing an intelligent thing.
10. *Energized*—You feel so energized that you are proud and supercilious. You are *bouncy*, so *bouncy* that you bounce around from thing to thing and don't complete anything. You feel so *curious;* everything captivates your attention that you forget your missions, operations, and objectives. You feel *hyper*—too *hyper*—to the point the people you are in charge of won't do their missions, operations, and objectives.

THE STRUCTURE OF PERSEVERANCE!

11. *Grateful*—You feel so grateful that you are indebted to someone. You feel so *gratified* that you fall in love with the person. You are *savoring* the emotion and feeling so much you are in a bubble of a stupor. You feel *thankful,* so *thankful* you feel indebted to the country or person.
12. *Helpless*—You feel so helpless that you think you can't do the missions, operations, and objectives. You feel so *baffled* that you are confused. You feel *challenged,* so *challenged* that you give up! You feel so *clueless* that you think you're hebetudinous.
13. *Hopeful*—You're so hopeful that something is going to happen you forget about anything else. You are *craving* something so much you are so infatuated with it, you are obsessed with it. You are *eager,* you forget about all the other factors. You are so *expectant* of something, you are in suspense for years.
14. *Hurt*—You hurt so much, you are afraid to do it. You can hurt so much that you can feel *humiliated.* You have been *stung* once, so you won't do it again. You have been *stung* doing your missions, operations, and objectives that you don't do them. You feel *tortured* that you feel that they are in charge.

15. *Insecure*—You feel so insecure that you are unstable or unbalanced! You cannot make a balanced decision. You feel so *bashful* that you don't have a high ego to get anything done. You feel *befuddled* or dumbfounded. You actually become cynical.
16. *Introspective*—You are introspective to the point you don't think about the enemy's efforts, your environment, or what your surroundings are. You're *contemplative* or indecisive. You are *engrossed*. You are so enlightened that you worship the person or country.
17. *Joyful*—You are so joyful that you don't understand the angle or premise that the country is coming at you with. You feel *amused*, hypnotized, or mesmerized. You feel totally *delirious*, totally confused! You feel so *euphoric* that you don't think rationally.
18. *Kind*—You are so kind, that everybody gets away with everything. You feel *cordial*. You feel *pitying* to the enemy or country. You feel *sympathetic* to the enemy or country.
19. *Loving*—You try to be such a loving person that your decisions for the country are the wrong ones; it promotes violence. You are *accepting*, so you accept everything even if it's bad for you, the country, or anybody.

THE STRUCTURE OF PERSEVERANCE!

You are *admiring*, you are mesmerized by everything. You are *devoted* to one thing—nothing else matters, like your missions, operations, and objectives!

20. *Sadness*—Your sadness is so great, you have no identity, ego, or superego. You feel *choked* by a gradually narrowing tunnel. You feel *defeated*, so defeated by how many losses you have, you give up. You feel *sorrowful* to the leader or country, so much now that the leader or country will defeat you.

21. *Surprised*—You're so surprised that it broke your concentration. You feel so *astonished* that you think the person or country is better than you or your country, which makes you feel defeated. You feel *scandalized*, like they outsmarted you. You feel stunned, and while you are *stunned*, they take advantage of you or your country by doing things that will defeat you.

22. *Unkind*—You are supposed to be the unkindest person on the planet, making your charisma as being that of an evil person. You feel cruel if you do something. You are so *greedy* they make you think you'll be defeated. The enemy makes you feel *immoral* to discredit you, affecting your identity, ego, and superego.

You are in bondage and imprisoned with your friends and family. You are in bondage and prison with your friends on social media. They got your signature; it's a very powerful move when somebody has your signature. If they have your signature you, will feel like they are in charge of you. Your leaders have your signature. Your friends and family are your leaders, or are you the leader of your friends and family? Make the choice. Your choice should be you are the leader of your friends and family! Your choice should be I'm the leader of my leaders. Be careful when you do that though. Your friends and family use all these emotions and feelings to get you do what they want you to do. Your leaders use all these emotions and feelings to get you to do what they want you to do. Emotions and feelings are beyond powerful, a signature is beyond powerful.

CHAPTER 8

A debate structure, an argument structure, and the structure of a conversation—these have three parts in them, like a triangle and like a syllogism. In a debate or argument, your conversation can go like this:

1. The other person says "His tax plan is the best!"
2. There are three things in that sentence; one is "His," two is "tax plan," and three is "best!"
3. You need a metaphor, the fourth object.
4. You say, "Your tax plan is like a lost person."
5. The metaphor is a "lost person."
6. You give facts of why his tax plan is like a "lost person."
7. You pierced his premise with a metaphor.
8. You punctured his premise with a metaphor.
9. Your original sentence has three things in it; one is "Your," two is "tax plan," and three is "lost person."

10. That is how you get penetration on the triangular premise.
11. You speak triangular. You should see how or what a conversation structure is now.

*Mnemonics have charisma. Objects have charisma. You have got to identify these charismas and write down, and it is necessary to use black spray paint and paint over what you wrote down or over the glow or glare, so you can concentrate.

Delta Force is the invisible force! Delta forces in the military are a force that is invisible because you can't determine who did it. It can be like motionless martial arts. Delta forces can invade your belongings by coming in on you and just moving an object in your living space by a millimeter. Delta forces will move it a millimeter to tilt the whole picture. Tilt what you are thinking. Delta forces can come in on you and do something to add weight to your picture in your head by placing dust or dirt on a surface in your living space. Your brain feels that, and your brain now thinks somebody else is in charge. You are not in charge anymore. Delta forces don't always kill people. Their operations can be mostly psychological warfare and political warfare, which are acts of war. The enemy has delta forces also. When that stuff happens, write down what happened. Visualize it or write it under one of the categories of the "Where you are at and what are you in" list.

Life is like a chess game. You move something, and if somebody moves it after you, your brains knows, but it makes them in charge, unless you identify what they did.

The tactic where people make you feel like you don't even know how to tie your shoes yet is a powerful angle and premise. They tell you that you need to be retrained. It is a powerful angle and premise. The tactic of self-inspections is powerful. Do the self-inspection anyway; it helps you on a new plan of attack. On-the-spot corrections are a polite way to say to somebody "You're doing something wrong!"

*Note: Every angle or premise that is in your environment is either psychological warfare (words) or political warfare (objects)! That is the best way to think about it for perseverance.

*Note: Identify what attacks your identity, ego, and superego.

A person who is successful is a person with a lot of leverage tools. The things that I list as they are attacking you with can be your leverage tools against them. You can use the tool "I have an open-door policy!" It would be a bottomless-pit gag on them!

Building models of things is a very positive thing for you to do. You can use popsicle sticks. You can use Legos. You can use several decks of cards. You can paint a painting. You can draw a drawing. You can write books of a model of what you want to accomplish. This would be positive motions.

What caused your emotions and feelings? What was the cause and what was the effect? What was the emotion and feeling that affected you and what did it make you do? You got to think about this stuff constantly. What made you have to desire to do that?

After reading this book, you will be able to write a crime report, and you will be able to write intelligence reports. Your reports will be extremely thorough, meticulous, professional-looking, and powerful.

If you want to be a leader, then move mountains. Just like playing the drums or a musical instrument, you strategically decide what mountain to move at what time. I most definitely want you to move mountains. This is what makes any country have more advanced inventions and makes it more prosperous.

When you do algebra, you can have a vortex. This is a diagram of what is vexing and what is perplexing in the most intense spot, the vortex.

THE STRUCTURE OF PERSEVERANCE!

In World War II, they used newsletters on the enemy. They dropped them out of bomber airplanes all over cities with millions and millions of newsletters to achieve a wide variety of things on the enemy. Newsletters are still powerful even, if you know it's a propaganda tool. It is still effective. They also used decoy men in the Battle of Normandy—the decoy tactic. Reaching for something and it turning out to be fake has a strong effect on you mentally, especially if you walk for miles or drive for miles to get to it.

The things you see on television that are doubles of something associated with or coincidences to things in your life are beyond powerful. They put you in a blurry zone or a zone of fog. They affect your brain. "Nobody controls what I say!"

Do you think it is important to pay attention in class now? Suck this all in like a sponge. Suck this whole book in like a sponge.

You don't want to hide your kids from violence. It has effects on them, like they won't be able to watch television news channels because they are too violent. They won't get a job as a doctor because it's too violent. They won't get a job as a lawyer because it's too violent.

Semantics are important. You actually construct semantics, so you can remember it later. The semantics in your living space need to be things that remind you of the past and future. So you have things on your note boards that remind you of what? An apple reminds you of a refrigerator and a full stomach. You eat this food, and you remember that it makes you feel good when you eat it. Popsicles remind you of a freezer; they make you think of the cold, and you remember how popsicles make you feel if it is hot out. If it's cold out, it reminds you of your warm home. If you think of water, you think many things all at once; you think of your kitchen, you think of your shower or bath. When you think of a cup of water, the water makes you think of a lot of things. Semantics in your environment get you to have determinism. Your fingernail is connected to your fingers. Your fingers are connected to your hand. If you want to remember something forever, you have got to have more than one semantic. You have got to construct more than one semantic to remind of that thing you want to remember forever. So the semantic, the 180-year calendar, reminds you of your life. The "wall of life" reminds you of your life. The "notebook of life" reminds of your life. Don't you want to remember your life? All these doctors want you to forget your life and forget your past. The doctors are the angle and premise of the professor category 19 of the list of "Where you are at and what you are in." You are conditioned, conformed, cultivated, and funneled to forget your past. You will have dead spots in your remembrance of the past. Figure out the dead spots; I gave you the tools to do it. Work those brain muscles. Never forget what makes you. Everybody has determinism. But if you control what is in your environment, then you will control what your determinism is. This will make it free will.

Say 1 million people are all watching the same television channel. Those same 1 million people are thinking the exact same thing at the exact same time (while they watch the same television channel). It is universal (meaning all), like Universal Studios. If those 1 million people see popcorn on that same television channel, those 1 million people all think of popcorn at the exact same time. After watching television today, what will they do tomorrow at the exact same time? They might think of the solution or answer to the television program they saw yesterday and have all people solve it at the same time. Subliminal messages sculpt the future, unless you have freewill thinking. If you write a fifty- to a hundred-page book, this will make you a better reader because you will understand what you got to do to design a book. You will get interested to read more books because you want to see the design of those books, magazines, and newspapers. You want to see the structure of the books, magazines, and newspapers. If you write the structure of sentences, you will be more exposed to different kinds of sentences. So you get more experience at writing and reading. It's like anything else you get experience at—you get better at it. The more you play the drums the better you get at it. The structure of perseverance is what? You want to remember this book forever, so you will have perseverance forever. So how do you do that? You make many semantics. The semantics that reminds you of this in the book. This semantic reminds me of that in the book. Construct a wall of semantics to remind you of the things in this book. Take the energy and time to do that. Use your brain muscles to do that. You want to have experience at more perseverance. You have got to have experience at using this book. Why don't you try that as a test for whether or not you have perseverance.

Reading a book out loud will make you a better reader. Reading a book out loud will get you to read a teleprompter better. It takes practice. Reading out loud will make you a better leader. Reading out loud will give experience as being a speaker. Reading out loud helps you with writing books. Reading out loud gives you better experience of working with punctuation in sentences. Read paragraphs in this book a couple of times out loud. If you read out loud, this is a way to create semantics to remember this book better.

Social media has a program called the Beacon Program. The Beacon Program collects data on you. The Beacon Program collects intelligence on you, on what you search for on your computer. Then they recircle it back to you. It's the double's angle and premise tactic. The double angle and premise of Category 21 in the "Where you are at and what are you in list." The Beacon Program collects data on you, intelligence on you, and recircles it back to you as coincidences, which is also an angle and premise of coincidences in category 21 of the "Where you are at and what are you in list." You have got be aware of this tactic. It's detrimental to the human being.

This is detrimental psychological warfare and detrimental political warfare. It's detrimental if it boxes you in mentally. If you see a box with your name on it, that is detrimental political warfare. If you see a circle with your name in it, that is detrimental political warfare. If you see a box with the words "I'm in here," that is detrimental political warfare. Saying the words "You are in the box!" is detrimental psychological warfare because you are using words to put the person or persons in the box.

These angles and premises can go under angle and premise category 23 of the "Where you are at and what are you in" list.

Perseverance is sending out newsletters, like they did in World War II—dropping millions of newsletters out of the plane to millions of people trying to hypnotize, mesmerize, conform, cultivate, and funnel them to get the enemy to do things, so we could win the war. Test yourself. Write up a one-page or half-a-page of a newsletter and send it out all over the country and all over the world. Send it to the same person every day for three years. Do you have the ego to do that? Do you have the morale to do that?

*Note: Cultivating somebody is like making a cult with them. Cultivating is using determinism on them. You have got to do this if you want to be a successful person. You have got to do it in a tactful manor though.

*Note This book gets you to think and interpret things in a different manor that is totally beneficial.

The Johari window is a structure of a box or square with four squares in it. You can look up the Johari window on the internet for free. It is a way to figure out the structure on your friends and family. I believe it is the structure for being creative and getting out of the black. You need as many tools as possible to stop your friends and family from funneling you into doing drugs and alcohol.

Everybody should get more experience on how chemicals change our body. If you get chemicals into the bloodstream just by touching soap, what can these toxins do? Well, your immune system has to react to these foreign chemicals that entered the bloodstream. One of the things it does is it steals things from your enzymes to fight the chemicals. This process drains your vitamin body makeup and makes you feel fatigued. When you're fatigued, you can't deal with anything. You can't deal with stress. Your brains neurons fire erratically, causing your body to steal more things from more enzymes, making you even more fatigued. Does this affect your morale? A prosperous country is a country that has a high morale. You have got to get these toxins out of your body. You need a good detoxing diet constantly and a detox kit every once in a while to keep you biology free of toxins.

*Note: You would think people would listen to an army tanker.

If everybody in the country—all five hundred million people—ran for a government office to represent the people, then nobody would do drugs and alcohol.

Cover your every move. People set you up for failure all the time. Scam artists do it all the time. You have got to be one step ahead at all times. You have got be one step ahead of the criminals at all times. How do you do that? The answers are in this book. Is the 180-year calendar one step ahead of everybody else? Yes, it is. That does not mean a scam artist won't get in on you. It's a constant battle of staying one step ahead.

The tool that keeps me from doing drugs and alcohol is the saying "Life is tough, but life is even tougher on drugs!"

Feelings and emotions go under category 23 of the "Where you are at and what are in" list. Friends and family use emotions and feelings on us. The friends and family angles and premises is in category 22 in the same list. Breaking it down like that into different categories is the divide and conquer method. The divide and conquer method has infinity equations and formulas. "I am going to divide and conquer this! I am going to divide and conquer that!" You divide and conquer the angles and premises. Whatever the force is, you divide it and conquer it. If you wave to a person or a crowd, this action also bonds you to that person or crowd. A handshake or wave funnels you. A handshake gets you to put your guard down. It bonds you to things.

It bonds you to them, making them look superior to you. This is angle and premise 22 in the "Where you are at and what you are in" list.

Ecosystems change your emotions and feelings. The chemicals change your biology. The chemicals affect your biology, just like drugs and alcohol. You're exposed to this ecosystem, and then you're exposed to that ecosystem of chemicals. It's a maze of ecosystem obstacles because each chemical changes your emotions and feelings in a different way. It affects morale. It affects your senses, so it keeps you in the fog and from identifying any angles or premises. It is a maze of emotions and feelings. Identify the ecosystems. This chemical causes this and this chemical causes that. Think cause and effect. How does this chemical affect me? Ecosystems weaken the enemy. Chemicals weaken the enemy. Identify what is weakening the enemy. Identify the ecosystems. Ecosystems are an angle and premise in category 30 in the "Where you are at and what you are in" list.

Weather affects morale. Weather has ecosystems in it. The military attacks when it's the right time. The military tracks weather for months ahead to have the right sequence of attacks, correlating with the weather. Everything is coordinated. Everything is orchestrated. The perfect storm. What is the perfect storm you are in? Using your "Where you are at and what are you" list, identify, identify, identify. Weather is in angle and premise category 30 of the list.

*Note: Pay attention to details!

Pollutions and toxins weaken the enemy, or they weaken us. Identify anything that weakens us or the enemy. Use psychological warfare and political warfare to weaken the enemy, and they will use it on us to weaken us. You can weaken the enemy by telling them the wrong foods to eat. The doctors in your own country can weaken us from within. It's called internal sabotage. Biological warfare and chemical warfare weaken us and the enemy. It is currently in the Geneva Convention to not use nuclear warfare, biological warfare, and chemical warfare. It's not just an act of war; it destroys agriculture, the living organisms, the dirt, and the ecosystems of the whole planet. The enemy doesn't care about that though. The enemy has equations with nuclear warfare, biological warfare, and chemical warfare. It's in their books of martial arts. It's a part of their culture to use nuclear warfare, biological warfare, and chemical warfare.

*Note: Identify what is weakening us.

*Note: Use lists and lists of mnemonics on your note boards or whatever is in your file cabinets and

THE STRUCTURE OF PERSEVERANCE!

your environment, because these ecosystems of previously used nuclear warfare, biological warfare, and chemical warfare are still in the air. These lists are there, so you won't forget to do your missions, operations, and objectives because of the exposure to these ecosystems.

How do your friends and family funnel you while these ecosystems affect us?

The real definition of a win-win situation is one where each side has things that they win, so both sides win—that is the real definition of win-win.

Can you stay moral with these ecosystems affecting us? This is why you do detox kits forever. Because you don't want to lose control of yourself from the exposure to the ecosystems.

When an actor gets slapped in the face, people talk to them, just like they talk with ordinary people. If you have kids, they talk, like you talk. It's the angle and premise of category 21 in the "Where you are at and what you are in" list.

Each vocabulary word is a tool, and you have got to have the right tool for the job. This why it's good to study vocabulary even after you die.

Life is about who has the most tools, so expose yourself to as many things as possible. You have an endless memory. Think of memory like this: memory files and compartments. You drive fifteen thousand miles, and you got compartments of memory files spread out over the fifteen thousand miles you traveled, like a condominium.

There are enemies in this country right now. They run missions, operations, and objectives on you to get you to do drugs and alcohol. Where do these drugs come from? Enemy countries. Drugs and alcohol destroy countries. Its' an act of war to deliberately destroy a country by getting people in the country hooked on drugs and alcohol. They run other missions, operations, and objectives here in this country also.

CHAPTER 9

Do you now know what a psychological operation is? A psychological operation is a mission or operation that the military or enemy runs on you. They can be in civilian clothes, not in military uniforms. Their mission is to use one of the categories from the "Where you are at and what are you in" list. They can also run a series of angles and premises from the same list. This is an equation. This is an algorithm. This is an orchestrated attack from the thirty categories of the list. They can use all thirty of them on you or just three. The military or enemy puts listening bugs and visual bugs in your vehicle, office, or home—and let's not forget they have listening devices that can hear through walls. They collect data from these devices on what you are saying. Social Media does it also. They can come at you with mirror images listed as the double's tactic or come up to you on the street and repeat what you said in your vehicle. This causes paranoia. It's psychological. They run a series of algorithms on you. A psychological operation is both psychological warfare with words and political warfare with charisma, objects, and colors, which affect your emotions and feelings. All along, you fight your way through the maze of ecosystems that also affect you. They can get you to do drugs and alcohol, so you won't complete you missions, operations, and objectives. These psychological operations are known to be Delta Force operations.

*Note: Identify if it's a threat or a friendly "Halt, who goes there? Advance to be recognized."

*Note: Identify what you're focused on.

*Note: Identify what's hypnotizing or mesmerizing you.

*Note: This book gives you tools to identify things. Use them. Break things down into categories. Divide and conquer.

*Note: A country that gives you free stuff is like a mama bird bringing the food, and you are indebted to mama bird for life. It's hypnotism.

*Note: The enemy wants you to feel defeated and think negative, put you in that type of coma, so you give up.

*Note: Go above and beyond.

*Note: All these angles and premises are like a telegraphed punch.

THE STRUCTURE OF PERSEVERANCE!

*Note: Each and every angle and premise of the "Where you are at and what are you in" list is extremely powerful, and you have got to use that list of thirty angles and premises every day—make it a habit.

*Note: Think triangular.

*Note: Missions, operations, and objectives.

*Note: Repeatedly say to yourself forever "I got to stay motivated!" and "I've got to stay focused."

*Note: Positive thoughts generate positive actions. Negative thoughts generate negative actions. Example, you've got to think you will be a millionaire because if you don't, it will never happen. Pretend you are the president of a corporation. You and all your corporate offices are thinking negative. Your environment is you, and your corporate officers are all saying "Our company is going under." If you think that way, your company will go under. Think positive. What is the environment of the president of a corporation?

*Note: Having perseverance is what makes people successful. Don't leave anything unfinished. Complete the mission. Complete the operation. Complete the objective. This also makes you organized. Honesty sends defeat. Send nothing but defeat.

*Note: You are a force of nothing but puncture.

*Note: Do you see how important it is for our military to know what is causing butterfly effects, vacuums, and funnels in foreign countries? Do you see how small the cause can be to start a butterfly effect, vacuum, and funnel?

*Note: If you do what is in this book, you will be unstoppable.

*Note: What does it take to do what is in this book—a crack to the jaw?

*Note: After reading this book, think about a homeless person.

*Note: What can you learn from your environment?

*Note: Fight your way through the fog with your pen.

*Note: I'll make a general out of you yet.

*Note: It's never too late to start.

*Note: Follow the line you are on, you're a straight arrow.

*Note: What environment or shuffleboard does the enemy have you standing on? You are always surrounded by the enemy, especially if you are in a free country.

*Note: What or whose theater are you in?

*Note: This book is like a creed.

*Note: You are Big Red 1 coming through.

THE STRUCTURE OF PERSEVERANCE!

*Note: I hope you suck in everything in this book like a sponge.

Even when this book ends, it never ends.

ABOUT THE AUTHOR

Stanley Slaczka is a Scorpio born on October 25, 1970. He was enlisted into the military in 1990. He served four years as an armored tank crew member. Among the tankers, this school is known as the University of General Patton. He served in Vilseck, Germany, under the First Armored Division, then the Third Infantry Division. He then moved back to the United States and served under Big Red 1 at Fort Riley, Kansas, First Infantry Division. He went to school at an automotive and diesel technical school called Rosedale. He then signed back into the army reserves and served under 319th Engineers and Second Medical Brigade. Some people say he resembles General Patton! While serving in Vilseck, Germany, the soldiers from the First Persian Gulf War came back and trained him. He was trained frequently throughout his military career. He plays the drums!

CPSIA information can be obtained
at www.ICGtesting.com
Printed in the USA
BVHW052322221022
649944BV00001B/67